"*Making Your Emotions Work for You* is a great book on how feelings can lead to spiritual defeat or guide us to a whole new life."

—**Steve Arterburn**, founder of Women of Faith and New Life Ministries and author of 70 books, including *Every Man's Battle*

"Harold Sala has not only given us the information we need to lead emotionally healthy lives—he has done it in profound yet easy-to-understand ways...Numerous fascinating illustrations...imprint how we really need to apply these truths in our everyday lives."

—**D. Ross Campbell, MD**, psychiatrist and author of the bestseller *How to Really Love Your Child*

"Harold Sala has the right combination of wisdom, experience, and biblical knowledge to tackle a topic that has been overworked by pop psychologists and underworked by the church."

—**Diane M. Komp, MD**, Chief of Pediatric Oncology, Yale University School of Medicine (retired) and author of *Why Me? A Doctor Looks at the Book of Job*

"Sensitive, realistic, and insightful...You will discover or rediscover that life can be 'bright and beautiful' through applying these biblical principles."

—**Dick Johnson**, Chaplain, CMC International Conference of Police Chaplains, Swedish American Health System

"Dr. Sala...integrates...psychological studies with his wide-ranging experience counseling and advising people of faith...I recommend this book to anyone who wants to glean from the wisdom and experience of Dr. Sala as they learn how to make their emotions work for them rather than against them."

—**L. Jarrett Richardson, MD**, psychiatrist with special interest in mental health of missionaries

"With his characteristic gentleness, warmth, and grace, Dr. Sala teaches and encourages us in this book about a complex and often neglected subject—emotions and the Christian life...He sets a course that takes us right toward the balanced view that is actually taught in the Bible."

—**Matthew Elliott, PhD**, author of *Feel the Power of Listening to Your Heart* and president of Oasis International

Making Your Emotions Work for You

HAROLD SALA

HARVEST HOUSE PUBLISHERS

EUGENE, OREGON

Cover by Left Coast Design, Portland, Oregon

Cover photo © Steve Terrill

MAKING YOUR EMOTIONS WORK FOR YOU
Revised edition of *Unlocking Your Potential*
Copyright © 1996/2009 by Harold J. Sala
Published by Harvest House Publishers
Eugene, Oregon 97402
www.harvesthousepublishers.com

Library of Congress Cataloging-in-Publication Data

Sala, Harold J.
  Making your emotions work for you / Harold Sala.
     p. cm.
  Originally published: Gresham, Or. : Vision House Pub., 1996.
  ISBN 978-0-7369-2573-0 (pbk.)
  1. Emotions—Religious aspects—Christianity. I. Title.
BV4597.3.S25 2009
248.4—dc22

2008049432

09 10 11 12 13 14 15 16 17 / BP-NI / 10 9 8 7 6 5 4 3 2 1

CONTENTS

Acknowledgments

I want to express my sincere thanks to Louise Calvert, Maynard Eyestone, and Louisa Ampil, my faithful administrative assistant, along with the help of Paul Gossard, editor at Harvest House Publishers, for their editorial improvements remedying the situation created by the possibility I skipped school the day the proper use of commas was discussed in English class.

Foreword

by Gary D. Chapman

Emotions are one of the underappreciated gifts of God. We often hear people say, "You can't trust your emotions." Or, "It's faith, not emotions." Or, "Emotions fluctuate, but God is unchangeable." There is truth in all of these statements, but that does not mean that emotions are unimportant. Imagine watching a football game without emotions. Watching a sunset, standing on the beach, or smelling a rose all stimulate emotions. The word *cancer* stimulates emotions, especially if the doctor is talking about you.

God made us with the capacity for emotions. In God's design, emotions were meant to help us process life in a positive manner. The emotion of fear may keep us from getting too close to the edge of a precipice. The emotion of anger may be the motivator for social reform. Feelings of grief may lead us to talk about the losses of life and find meaning beyond the loss.

Emotions are not designed to control our lives, but to draw our attention to life. Positive emotions help us enjoy life, while negative emotions inform us that something needs attention. The problem is that we often act irresponsibly in response to our emotions and make things worse— sometimes much worse. That is why the Scriptures warn, "In your anger, do not sin" (Ephesians 4:26). The same warning would apply to any emotion. For example: "When you are fearful, don't sin." Or, "When you feel joyful, sad, excited, depressed, elated, or overwhelmed, do not sin."

For the Christian, there is always a proper response to emotions. The Scriptures give clear guidance. For example, David said, "When I am afraid, I will trust in the Lord." David did not deny his fear. Nor was he pushed by fear to flee. Rather, he took his fear to God, knowing that

His power was greater than whatever stimulated the fear. Thus, David chose to trust God and do what was right. The emotion of fear revealed that there was an enemy, but godly thought and action led him to victory over the object of fear.

In *Making Your Emotions Work for You,* Harold Sala gives a clear, biblical understanding of emotions and how we are to respond to them. This book will save the average Christian hundreds of hours of research. I am honored to write a foreword to such a practical guide to understanding and processing emotions.

—Gary D. Chapman
Author of *The Five Love Languages*
and *Love as a Way of Life*

Finding God's Plan
for Your Emotions

Pogo, a comic-strip character, and his friends decide to go to war. They sally forth against the enemy, their swords drawn, their spears readied. With lines of grim determination on their faces they are ready to attack.

Then the cartoonist pictures Pogo and his friends returning from the battle, which didn't take place, discouraged and disillusioned. Their swords are sheathed, their spears are dragging in the dust behind them. The caption reads, *"We have met the enemy, and he is us!"*

What Pogo discovered is exactly what I, sometimes painfully, have learned about myself! The greatest enemies are not the ones out there somewhere, lurking in the dark, awaiting the proper moment to attack me. Rather, they are the ones within.

The greatest struggles in life are not fought on the battlefields of the world; they are fought in human hearts as we struggle with issues such as frustration, stress, lack of self-confidence, fear, feelings of inadequacy and inferiority, and the inability to cope with circumstances that are not to our liking.

While these challenges can defeat you—and they do defeat many people, or at least reduce their effectiveness in life and level of fulfillment and happiness—they can also serve as catalysts to bring out the very best in you.

Making Your Emotions Work for You is written with this purpose in mind. None of us chooses the circumstances or the time of his birth. We only make choices as to how we respond to the circumstances that confront us—choices that either make us or break us. In this book I have not attempted to define all of our inner struggles from the perspective of the latest pop psychology or what's hot in the marketplace of trends and ideas. Rather, I have chosen to confront some of the issues facing us today and discuss how to cope with them—no, how to make them work for you, applying scriptural principles that unleash God's enabling power in your personal life. The abiding principle is that He who crafted and gifted us, giving us individuality and uniqueness, knows how we can best find His purpose and fulfill His calling, accomplishing what He wants us to do. This is what Paul described when he said he wanted "to lay hold of that for which Christ Jesus has also laid hold" of him.

I acknowledge that I approach the subject with a measure of bias that has come through years of working with people and from a deep confidence that God is a good God and that His Word is trustworthy—a marvelous book with deep, profound insights into our lives including our emotions. It is with that conviction that I take you on this journey, showing you how you can make your emotions work for you—and in the process, how you can actually make friends of your emotions so the end result is that you become a more positive, confident, fulfilled person.

Harold Sala

Mission Viejo, California

CHAPTER 1

Understand Yourself—
You're Worth the Bother

For an attractive account executive, it began as a rather routine business trip—a three-hour flight followed by the taxi ride to the hotel, then dinner with industry colleagues and drinks at the bar.

But what took place after that had never happened before, wasn't planned, and was completely unexpected. The woman I am describing responded to the overtures of a fellow executive and, without thinking of the consequences of what she was doing, first allowed herself to be flattered, then to be embraced, then to become intimate with a man who was slightly more than a stranger.

What took place was totally out of character for this late-thirties woman, who was loved by an adoring husband, was the mother of two children, and attended church with her family on a regular basis. That brief encounter with passion came with a high price tag. She lost her job with a major U.S. corporation and almost lost her husband. Blame it on the alcohol or a lapse in judgment—the result of thinking, "What happens in Vegas stays in Vegas"—but for the rest of her life she will be asking herself the question, *Why did I do that?*

Yet are there not times when every single person does something—though perhaps not with the same consequences—and asks themselves the same question? Making this personal, have you ever had the experience of doing something—perhaps without really thinking or possibly with a great deal of forethought—and later scratching your head as you asked yourself, *What in the world possessed me to do that?* Or, *Why did I do such a thing? I really knew better than that!*

But at the time, under those circumstances, you did what your emotions prompted you to do. Or at least, you did what you wanted to do. Perhaps you reasoned, *Everybody is doing it.* Or you may have even thought, *Hey, if God placed that desire in my body, fulfilling it can't be displeasing to Him.* You may have reasoned, *Surely God wouldn't want me to be lonely!* trying to avoid personal responsibility for what you were doing.

> The more you know about what makes you tick, the more you will be in control of your life.

Later you looked back and regretted the decision you made. You anguished, saying, "I knew better. Why couldn't I control my emotions and passions?" I'm not suggesting for a moment that you go about psychoanalyzing yourself, but I am saying that the better you understand yourself, the greater will be the measure of happiness and fulfillment you have in life.

Loneliness, anger, frustration, stress, peer pressure, passions, the desire to please both man and God are all factors in your behavior, and the more you know about what makes you tick, the more you will be in control of your life.

Socrates was credited with the simple maxim *Know thyself.* The wise man of Athens was among the many to ponder the relationship of emotions to behavior, and taught his disciples that self-knowledge is a prerequisite to a deep understanding of life! But Socrates wasn't the first to look within his heart and ponder the mystery of life and human behavior.

At least six centuries before Socrates, a wiser man, David, king of Israel, pondered the nature of humankind as he wrote, "When I consider your heavens, the work of your fingers, the moon and the stars, which you have set in place, what is man that you are mindful of him, the son of man that you care for him?" (Psalm 8:3-4). David wasn't the only writer of Scripture who contemplated the complexity of human nature in an attempt really to understand himself. The Old Testament book of Proverbs is a collection of wisdom literature which was compiled about the time of Solomon, and in this book there is an underlying theme of man's attempt to discover his true nature.

In recent days, psychology, as one of the branches of behavioral science, has delved into the mind of man to help us better understand our behavior. The word *psychology* comes from two Greek words, *psuche,* meaning "soul," and *logos,* meaning "a word" or "the study of." Hence, modern psychology is the study of man's nature and behavior. While the study of psychology does provide us certain insights into ourselves, an even deeper understanding of ourselves and our natures comes through God's textbook on life and living, the Bible, which came through the inspiration of the Holy Spirit.

Is it worth the time and effort to try to understand yourself and the pressures and forces which contribute to your behavior? Indeed it is! If you are a parent—married or single—with emotional needs in your life which are not met, in all probability you will be frustrated, and that frustration may well contribute to relationships and situations which are not in your best interest. Furthermore, not understanding what your emotional needs are and how they can best be met may also mean that your children grow up with blind spots in their lives. Understanding yourself is the first step toward being a better parent.

You Are a Unique Individual— An Original Without Duplication

Today we hear a lot about *individualism.* But when it gets down to the bottom line, most of us are not "rugged individualists" at all. We are pressure-cooked into bland uniformity with everyone else, and we tend to think of someone who is independent and thinks for himself as something quaint or odd. We don't want to be different, so we conform to a kind of cookie-cutter pattern that defines our values in terms of our culture rather than striving to let our values determine the framework of our lives and our relationship to our culture.

God made you an individual, and in these days of mass everything, we seem to have lost sight of the fact that individuality resulted from God's design. When you were conceived, some 200 to 300 million sperm competed with each other to fertilize the ovum that made you what you are. Only one succeeded. Thus, by virtue of the unique arrangement of your genes and chromosomes at conception, the 10-plus trillion cells in your body are put together a bit differently from those in all of the other 6.9 billion people here on earth.

Seldom do we ever think about how many and how complicated the systems are that function within our bodies. Every seven years, your body replaces its trillions of cells with new ones, in a process that gradually slows as you age. Your brain is an amazing organ, which serves as the nerve center of your body. Should you have the misfortune of sitting on a tack, a message is immediately transmitted to your brain via a network of nerves. Your brain, in turn, formulates an expression of pain, which your vocal cords express in no uncertain terms, and all of this takes place almost instantaneously.

Yale University psychologist Dr. Neal Miller described the human brain as the most complex organ on earth, containing 100 billion cells, or neurons. Each of these is connected with 10,000 billion other nerves.[1] No computer has ever been invented that even comes close to rivaling the complexity of your brain. Never do you have to say, "Brain cell number 222,334, get to work; you aren't carrying your load." It's automatic!

Your body has an amazing air-conditioning system that adjusts to your environment. Your skin has more than two million tiny sweat glands on its surface—about 300 per square inch—that keep your body regulated at an even temperature.

Your heart, slightly larger than a man's fist, pumps 1800 gallons of blood through 60,000 miles of veins, capillaries, and arteries every day—24/7. In your stomach are 35 million glands secreting juices to aid the process of digestion, acids strong enough to take varnish off a table, yet working harmlessly in your body.

All of this we take for granted. Now, see how this applies to you as an individual. Nobody else thinks with your mind. Neither does anyone else see with your eyes or hear with your ears, walk with your legs or hold things with your hands. No one else in the entire world feels exactly what you feel. You are one of a kind, without duplication. The blend of emotions and feelings within you is unique. These emotions and feelings cannot be displayed on a screen, x-rayed, or dissected in a laboratory. They are part of your uniqueness, given to you at the moment you were conceived, as DNA from two parents came together.

Your vantage point is different from that of everyone else in our world. There is tremendous freedom in accepting the fact that you don't have to be pressured into conformity with everybody else—that you can be yourself, an individual created in the image of God with sensitivity and personality that came from His design.

A retired army officer, the father of twelve children—six sons and six daughters—began to tell me about his children and how no two were exactly alike. "Each one," he reflected, "is different from the rest. Though they are alike in some ways, when you consider them individually, each is unlike any other."

Diamonds, emeralds, and rubies are all precious stones, yet they have properties and characteristics which make them unique and different. No two diamonds are exactly alike. Their color, cut and clarity all define them. So is it with individual differences in a family. Two children may have the same parents, be raised in the same family, and even share friends in common, yet those two may be vastly unlike each other in many ways.

Today we badly need to understand that it's okay to be you—an individual created in the image of God with emotions, gifts, and talents that no one else has in exactly the same mix.

You Are a Spiritual Being

The second fact that will help you understand yourself is to recognize that you are an individual who has a spiritual nature. This is one area where much of modern psychology and psychiatry has had a blind spot. Many psychologists and psychiatrists don't recognize that man is more than a highly developed mammal, but rather he is essentially a spiritual being made in the image of God and, therefore, has a spiritual nature.

The Bible says it is your spiritual and moral nature that sets you apart from lower forms of life. But when you lose sight of that spiritual nature, your conduct may well take on characteristics of those who live as though there is no God and no accounting of our actions to Him.

Down through the centuries men and women, in different ways, have described the barrenness of the empty life that comes when the spiritual nature of our lives is ignored. Augustine, in the fourth century, wrote that the human heart is restless until it finds itself in God. Blaise Pascal, the French philosopher, originated the idea of the God-shaped vacuum, that yearning for fulfillment and wholeness in the heart of every person, which can be filled only by Jesus Christ.

If you really want to understand yourself, then realize that you're not a highly evolved animal; rather, you are a human being who has complex emotional and spiritual needs that cannot be separated into neat compartments. As I will demonstrate in subsequent chapters, your emotions affect your spiritual life, and your spiritual life powerfully affects your sense of right and wrong, your feelings of guilt or compliance with the will of God.

The entire story of redemption is actually a very simple one, the story of how sin or rebellion estranged man from his Creator, and how a loving Father sent His Son to bridge the gulf between us and Himself and bring us back into fellowship with Him. Isaiah, the prophet of old, put it, "We all, like sheep, have gone astray, each of us has turned to his own way" (Isaiah 53:6).

The fact that something happened to our spiritual life back in our first father Adam explains a lot of things in the world. It explains how Adolf Hitler could send fourteen million people (six million Jews and eight million Gentiles) to their deaths in the concentration camps of Europe, how Pol Pot could snuff out the lives of two to three million innocent victims in Cambodia (1975 to 1980), and how the same kind of evil in human hearts could annihilate millions of people in Bosnia-Herzegovina and Rwanda. But it also explains a great deal about your personal life today, things you would prefer to ignore, or at least minimize.

It explains how a husband can be unfaithful to a wife who dearly loves him, and vice versa. It explains how at times we all find ourselves doing things we know are wrong, but enjoy doing them anyway.

Paul talked about this conflict in our natures when he wrote Romans chapter 7. Probably you can identify with him:

> I don't understand myself at all, for I really want to do what
> is right, but I can't. I do what I don't want to do—what I
> hate. I know perfectly well that what I am doing is wrong,
> and my bad conscience proves that I agree with these laws I
> am breaking (Romans 7:15-16 TLB).

Paul is saying that the very things he didn't want to do were the things that he did, and the very things he did want to do were the things he left undone. He characterized the despair of a lot of people when he wrote, "What a wretched man I am! Who will rescue me from this body of death?" (Romans 7:24).

That's part of the reason why at times you are torn between doing things you know will hurt another and doing what is right. You feel incapable of helping yourself, so you begin to resent yourself and wish you were different. In that same passage Paul says that you can be different because of the power of God's Holy Spirit; he writes in Romans 8:1, "Therefore, there is now no condemnation for those who are in Christ Jesus."

As a believer you can stand in the presence of God, justified—free of the guilt of your sins—because you have been forgiven. Paul put it like this:

> God made him [Christ] who had no sin to be sin for us,
> so that in him we might become the righteousness of God
> (2 Corinthians 5:21).

It doesn't mean, however, that the age-old struggle of the flesh and the Spirit will not be with you until the end of time. It will. The difference is that as God's child, there comes an enabling (the power of Christ within you) that makes it possible for you to live in such a way that you are in harmony with God's will.

The mentality of our day is that God expects far too much of us, more than we are capable of delivering (in other words, He doesn't really mean what He says). But the good news of the gospel is that your life can be different, enriched, and enabled because of God's indwelling power.

You Are a Person of Great Value

May I ask you a personal question? Do you like yourself? Or secretly—or maybe not so secretly—would you like to be someone else? On one occasion Winston Churchill was asked, "If you could not be who you are, who would you want to be?" He paused, then reached down and took his wife Clementine's hand and stroked it affectionately saying, "I would like to be Lady Churchill's second husband." Good answer.

Vast numbers of us are not always comfortable with ourselves, and in the U.S. this results in the spending of $20 billion a year on cosmetics, $300 million a year on plastic surgery, and $33 billion a year on dietary products (mostly to help you lose weight and get in shape).[2]

Why don't you like yourself? There are a variety of reasons to choose from: You can say...

- I don't like the way I look.
- I don't like my figure.
- I'm just a nobody.
- I'm not as gifted as some.
- My personality isn't as good as so-and-so's.
- I don't have the brains that he has.
- I can't think of clever things to say.
- I'm not funny.

There is no limit to the extent to which you can be unhappy with yourself and about yourself if you really try.

A listener to my radio program *Guidelines for Family Living* wrote the following: "I have a sister who is very petite and flat-chested, and this upsets her very much. She can't accept the fact that there are a lot more pretty clothes for small women than for big women. Her husband loves her very much and so do her children, but she has this hang-up about her body."

Women are not the only ones who are unhappy with themselves. Quite typical is the way one man described himself: "I am a disabled man with a spine disorder…always living in pain and weakness. Sometimes, I wonder why the Lord lets me suffer and endure this kind of life. I am ridiculed and mocked by others due to my ugly figure. No one really understands me, not even my wife."

When you are not happy with yourself, you won't be happy with others, because you will see in them the faults that you resent in yourself. And when you are not happy with yourself, you're not happy with God either, because you reason, *He made me like I am—so it is really His fault that I am like I am.*

As I write this I'm thinking of a teenage girl who attempted to take her life on a couple of occasions. She was actually rather pretty, but she didn't see it that way. She not only hated herself, but also disliked almost everybody else, too—her parents, her teachers, and a lot of her contemporaries. About the only friends she had were a few angry and rebellious teenagers who were very much a reflection of herself. Heavy-metal music that was nihilistic, alcohol, drugs, and sex were trips she had taken in her escape from reality, trying to find some meaning to the puzzle of life. She was gradually self-destructing.

Today, however, she is a different person because she came face-to-face with the fact that our rebellion against ourselves is really rebellion against God, and that we are the only ones who can respond to His love and cooperate with Him in making ourselves what we ought to be. Her life did a radical about-face, and she became a young woman with a future.

In the last decade, plastic surgery along with generous infusions of silicon and Botox have reinforced the thinking that equates self-worth with a more beautiful body. We have bought into the sexually saturated culture of our day that demands that women take out those wrinkles, get rid of that excess fat, enlarge their breasts, and do whatever is necessary to make themselves attractive to members of the opposite sex. Men are also told that surgical enhancement is the way to really please a woman. We have bought into the mentality that mandates spending hundreds of millions paying for elective cosmetic surgical procedures, and now we have begun to realize that they may boomerang on us and produce a fallout of hideous as well as devastating consequences.

Do Yourself a Favor—Love Yourself As You Are

Is it really wrong to like yourself just as you are? Going one step further, to humbly *love* yourself? Asking that question brings to mind an image of a proud, arrogant individual with a grossly inflated opinion of his own worth, right? That's not what I'm driving at. You have probably been taught that if you are to be able to love others you must depreciate yourself and crucify your flesh. True, in writing to the Galatians Paul talked about dying to self—the old fleshly nature—so that Christ may live; but this is totally different from putting yourself down and denigrating your value in God's sight.

Jesus taught that love would be the one indisputable evidence that God has touched our lives (John 13:34-35). He also instructed us that we are to love God supremely and love our neighbor as ourselves. He was very plain that one of the hallmarks of Christianity is the love believers have for each other, a love unlike that of individuals who do not know Christ—a love that results from the Holy Spirit's indwelling presence in our lives. However, one of the reasons God's love doesn't flow through some individuals to anyone else is that it is bottled up by feelings—feelings that range from a mild dislike to the downright hatred some people have for themselves. Understanding who you are and what your value is in the sight of God gives you freedom to love others. It's that simple.

Paul says that we ought not to think of ourselves more highly than is proper (Romans 12:3), but the inverse truth is just as meaningful: If you think of yourself *less* highly than you should, you are just as wrong.

> Your ability to love is vitally affected by the way you think about yourself.

Jesus' statement in Matthew 22:39 that we are to love our neighbor as ourselves recognizes that an understanding of who you are and a recognition of your gifts and abilities bring a security that comes from within. It is essential if you are ever to learn to love your neighbor.

Even so, the concept of loving your neighbor as yourself didn't originate with Jesus in His ministry on earth. Long before, Moses faithfully recorded God's command: "Do not seek revenge or bear a grudge against one of your people, but love your neighbor as yourself" (Leviticus 19:18).

If you don't develop a humble measure of love for yourself, you will never be very successful in loving anyone else. As Soren Kierkegaard put it,

> When the commandment to love one's neighbor is rightly understood, it also says the converse, "Thou shalt love thyself in the right way." If anyone, therefore, will not learn from Christianity to love himself in the right way, then neither can he love his neighbor...To love one's self in the right way, and to love one's neighbor, are absolutely analogous concepts, and are at the bottom one and the same.[3]

In his book *Peace of Mind,* Joshua Liebman went even further in recognizing the impossibility of loving others when negative feelings of self-dislike or hate are present:

> He who hates himself, who does not have a proper regard for his own capacities...can have no respect for others. Deep within himself, he will hate his brothers when he sees in them his own marred image. Love for oneself is the foundation of a brotherly society and personal peace of mind.[4]

Your ability to love is vitally affected by the way you think about yourself. I'm thinking of individuals I have worked with who told me how their parents had cursed them and berated them with comments such as these:

"You're no good!"

"You've got bad blood in you!"

"You're the dumbest kid in the family!"

"You're a bastard—not my son!"

And the youngster began to visualize himself or herself as a loser, a person of little value, a mistake that should never have come into the world. What self-confidence there may have been quickly began to erode, and eventually those harsh words became a self-realizing prophecy.

The *Los Angeles Times* carried a front-page story of child abuse. A five-year-old boy was "hung by his hands and wrists from a door jamb and beaten with some sort of leash or chain...routinely denied food and water, burned with cigarettes on his body and genitals, and left to sit in his own urine and feces."[5]

Starkeisha Brown, the boy's 24-year-old mother, inflicted wounds that will forever scar and disfigure the little boy. "It causes you to question the humanity of some people," said Assistant Police Chief Earl Paysinger, "whether they have a heart or a soul."

Yes—that act is repulsive, horrible, unthinkable, and criminal, and the emotional abuse inflicted on some children scars them within and inflicts emotional damage that will haunt them for the rest of their lives.

God knows that all of us wrestle with enough negative feelings without having them hammered into our heads. To realize, however, that you can change with God's help, that God performs plastic surgery of the emotions, that He is the healer of broken hearts, lives, and bodies, that you don't have to live in a prison of inadequacy and inferiority, that you don't have to let circumstances destroy your future, is the first step toward becoming the kind of person you feel God would have you be and you would like to become.

You Are Capable of Change

First, let me point out that some people take refuge in failure. It is far easier for them to feel sorry for themselves and cry over their misery than assume a responsible plan of change. So year after year they tell other people about their difficulties and their failures. They are like walking clouds of gloom and doom, ready to tell you how they have been victimized by life. They'll tell you how their husband walked out and left them with nine children and that they are absolutely helpless because of the misfortunes that befell them. And you know something—they convince themselves! They take real delight in recounting the sordid details of their misery. Don't be one of them!

It is a fact that when a wayward husband really changes—turns his back on the habit or whatever was so repulsive to his wife and is soundly converted to Jesus Christ—instead of rejoicing, his wife often has great difficulty handling the change. Why? She no longer gets "Aw, isn't that terrible" responses from her friends.

William Glasser is a psychiatrist who has broken with the traditional approach to psychotherapy. He has developed an approach to the treatment of mental problems that is quite consistent with what Scripture says when it comes to the effects of our failures. Glasser says that the past doesn't have to destroy your future. In fact he refuses to listen to the sordid details of people's failures. "Psychiatric garbage" is the term he uses to describe the endless recounting of our troubles. Rather, he focuses on the fact that a lot of people suffer from "paralysis of analysis," as he describes it. They are doing nothing to change their lives and they want nothing done, but they are willing to spend endless hours talking about how they got into trouble. Talk is cheap and a lot easier than working to bring change.

Let me summarize by saying that if you are to change your life and the circumstances, three things are necessary: 1) the desire to change; 2) a commitment to change; and 3) follow-through. Change involves the cooperation of man and God, your working with the Spirit of God, being sensitive to His voice as He works out your Father's will in your life. Try to do everything in your own strength and you won't get very far, for you will very soon discover the weakness of human resolutions and good intentions. A lot of others before you, perhaps even stronger than you, have tried to turn over a new leaf, and their attempt at reformation resulted in producing another soiled page in the book of their life.

The greatest force in all the world when it comes to personality and behavioral changes is the Holy Spirit, who works in the life of the believer to bring him into conformity with God's plan and purpose. But this change or power is activated only by man's complete cooperation with the divine. An individual's determination to stay in the prison of self-pity or despair short-circuits the restorative work of the Holy Spirit. So if you are stuck in your cave of inadequacy and inferiority, pry yourself loose and get moving in a new direction, God's direction.

Do you fully believe you can be different? Instead of being angry with the world because you aren't six inches taller than you are, that you don't exactly have an hourglass figure, that your physique doesn't mirror that of Arnold Schwarzenegger, or whatever, you can work in harmony with the Holy Spirit in developing the kind of personality that lifts you six inches higher, that reveals integrity and strength within, that reflects the handiwork of God both inside and out. Gradually the light comes on—you are one of a kind, a creation of the Almighty, and it's okay to be *you*!

One more thing needs to be said in this chapter. If you happen to be disadvantaged by growing up in a home where you were neglected or abused, or you have had certain failures in your life that have stunted your emotional development, the longer you live with a loser complex, the more difficult it becomes to break out of the pattern of negative thinking that has imprisoned you.

The longer you live with negative situations and emotions, the more comfortable you become with them, and the more effectively they ensnare you. Do you remember the plight of Dr. Manette in Charles Dickens's *Tale of Two Cities*? Though Manette is liberated by the French Revolution and is eventually free to leave the hated Bastille, where he was imprisoned, he can't handle the freedom. He is secure only at his cobbler's bench, where he spent day after day as a prisoner.

That's why breaking out of the box that has imprisoned you and becoming the person God intended you to be is so very important.

∽

Having determined that your life can be different, you must make peace with yourself. The next chapter shows you how to accept yourself as you understand your true value and worth. Remember, you are your own worst enemy.

QUESTIONS FOR THOUGHT AND DISCUSSION

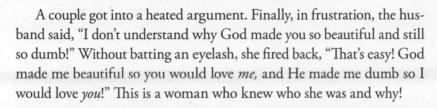

A couple got into a heated argument. Finally, in frustration, the husband said, "I don't understand why God made you so beautiful and still so dumb!" Without batting an eyelash, she fired back, "That's easy! God made me beautiful so you would love *me,* and He made me dumb so I would love *you!*" This is a woman who knew who she was and why!

1. Humor aside, what effect would her husband's words have had on the wife if she had really believed she was dumb? How might she have worked to overcome those insecurities?

2. What are two negative opinions you used to have of yourself that are no longer true, at least to the degree they used to be? How did you learn to decrease the effect they had on your life?

3. What are two negative characteristics you still see at work in your life? Try to take a clear, objective look at yourself. In what ways, if any, are you choosing to stay *stuck*? What are

three ways you can take action to change those characteristics or opinions?

4. To love yourself, according to Scripture, is to take care of
   yourself physically, emotionally, and spiritually so you have
   something to give to others. What is one way you can take
   care of yourself in each of those areas today?

This Will Hurt...

We are more likely to react than to respond when someone says something negative about us, especially when that person is an important part
of our lives. There are two reactions that are hurtful—either to yourself
or to the other person.

First, you may simply believe what the other person says and use that
as fuel in the fire of self-degradation. Your habit may be to simply accept
what other people say and beat yourself up for being that way. There is
little motivation to change if you don't believe it's possible.

The second hurtful reaction is to lash out—maybe with angry words,
maybe with complete denial. Some people refuse to see that they have
any problems at all. Deep inside, though, they feel the punches, and they
harbor the hurt.

Either reaction will always compound your feelings of insecurity.

This Will Help...

Someone once told Abraham Lincoln that one of his generals called him a fool. He replied, "Well, then, I must be one, because he is almost always right."

When you are hit with a criticism, it will help to stop a moment and consider that the person might have a point. You build the security to do this when you know that, as God's child, He sees you as a person of infinite value and worth. If the dig has even the smallest bit of truth to it, this might be motivation for you to work on that area of life. But if you have taken an honest look at yourself and you know that he is way off base, let it go. Vance Havner, a Southern evangelist of a previous generation, used to say, "Any bulldog can whip a skunk, but it just ain't worth it." Sometimes you have to let things go with the same mind-set. Reacting is not worth the cost to yourself or to the relationship.

CHAPTER 2

Answering the Question—
Who Am I?

A television station sent a reporter and crew out on the street to interview people. The reporter asked just one question: "Who are you?" In order to make the research valid the person was asked to give the first three answers that came to mind. Then what the person said was evaluated as to its psychological and social implications.

If an individual replied, "I'm a man!" or "I'm a woman!" that individual was thought to be conscious of his or her sexual identity.

If a woman answered, "Oh, I'm just a housewife," researchers concluded that she was unaware of the importance of her role as a wife and mother.

If a man replied, "I'm an executive, a stockholder, and a family man," it was believed that he was aware of his position in life, his social status, and his marital obligations.

If you were walking in the mall and a reporter from a local television station put a microphone in your face and asked, "Who are you?" how would you answer?

That there is a problem with identity today is borne out by the fact that nearly every women's magazine on the newsstand has an article or two about discovering your identity. I hasten to add that women aren't the only ones faced with this problem. Vast numbers of men, especially those who have been highly paid executives, get laid off and suddenly their image is scrimmaged. No longer do they don their pricey business suits and commute to the office with highly polished leather briefcase in hand. No. They stay at home. They scour the want ads. They hesitantly apply for unemployment benefits. No longer are they major contributors to the family's income, and they face an identity crisis of major proportions. Should they be asked, "Who are you?" they would be uncertain how to answer. "I used to be..." would not be an uncommon answer at all.

When we lack a clearly defined sense of identity, we feel inadequate, uncertain, and insecure. This can lead to one of two extremes. One extreme is that feelings of inadequacy lead to an *inferiority complex*. On the other hand, they may cause an individual to push too hard, trying to demonstrate how good he or she really is, an overcompensation which produces a *superiority complex*. If you really are good, you don't have to tell people. They know!

One of the primary reasons we have difficulty accepting ourselves and having a positive mental image of ourselves is that we do not understand how important we are in the sight of God. Failing to sense our importance before Him, the trickle-down effect eventually means we consider ourselves to be of little, if any, practical value. We feel shame and deficiency as a human being; and part of this is a feeling of inferiority and inadequacy.

Have you ever asked yourself, *How does God look at my life? Am I important to Him, and does what happens to me really make any difference to Him? Then, if I am important to Him,* how *important am I anyway?*

In His ministry, Jesus never lost sight of the importance of a single person, no matter how lowly or insignificant that individual's position was in life. In fact, some of His most profound theological discourses came as the result of conversations He had with individuals who were considered unimportant by society at large.

Consider the importance of what Jesus said about His Father's will following the conversation at the well of Sychar with a woman who was a social outcast. At the time, the disciples were astonished—not only at the fact that Jesus talked to a woman, but also that the woman was a Samaritan—and in all probability a woman of ill-repute since she drew water at high noon, whereas *virtuous* women came early or late in the day (see John 4).

What of the beautiful passage stressing forgiveness, which came from Jesus' encounter with an adulterous woman—a woman seized in the very act? Instead of reaching for a stone, Jesus extended compassion and forgiveness. "Go now and leave your life of sin" was His direction (see John 8:1-11).

When Jesus dealt with individuals, He looked beyond the veneer that produces social isolation amid peer groups that refuse to cross ethnic and social barriers. He disregarded custom and tradition. He saw value in each person with whom He came in contact—something that greatly distressed the Pharisees.

You Are a Person of Worth and Value in God's Sight

Jesus' attitude toward the individual was a reflection of His Father's attitude, which is revealed in the pages of the Old Testament and amplified by the writings of the New Testament.

The apostle Paul in particular gave insights as to the individual's worth when he wrote to the Ephesians and stressed that it was the sacrifice of Christ that enabled God not only to forgive us but to accept us and receive us as His adopted children. In the first few paragraphs of that Ephesian letter, he stressed several facts regarding the believer:

- God has chosen us before creation (1:4).

- God has adopted us into His family (1:5).

- God has accepted us in Christ (1:6).
- God has forgiven us because of the blood that was shed (1:7).

An understanding of these simple truths is necessary if you are to understand your value and worth in God's sight. Knowing and believing that God accepts you on the basis of what Jesus did for you is the key to a healthy self-image. Though modern translations more accurately render the text of Ephesians 1:6, the King James translators captured the truth and essence of what Paul was saying when they gave us these words: "He [God] hath made us accepted in the beloved [Christ]."

In life, your acceptance is based largely upon three factors: 1) appearance; 2) performance; and 3) influence. Appearance: Notice who gets waited on first in a department store—an elderly, slightly overweight woman, or a young, vivacious, very pretty young woman? Performance: It is the student with the highest grades who is admitted to the best college. Influence: The young man whose dad is influential and has money is the one who gets appointed to the team, not necessarily the boy who grew up in poverty who, nonetheless, is the better athlete.

> When your concept of God's forgiveness is deficient, you can never fully accept the truth that He has forgiven you.

This is the way it is. But unlike what we have come to accept as "the way it is," the Bible teaches that acceptance before God is never based upon your appearance or performance, or negative or positive influence. Because we in general believe that God is good, we tend to think that if we are "good enough" He will be impressed and accept us. Actually, your essential goodness, or your lack of it, has nothing to do with God's accepting you. "He saved us, not because of righteous things we had done, but because of his mercy. He saved us through the washing of rebirth and renewal by the Holy Spirit" (Titus 3:5).

The gospel is good news because it proclaims that no self-improvement program is necessary before you can come to the Father for forgiveness and help. Scores of individuals, however, are crippled emotionally by the popular belief that God accepts only those who are good—that at the end of the trip, He draws a line, and if your good deeds outnumber the bad, then and only then will He receive you and forgive you.

When your concept of God's forgiveness is deficient, you can never fully accept the truth that He has forgiven you. And being uncertain of your relationship with Him, you find it difficult or impossible to forgive yourself as well.

From a biblical perspective, understanding God's point of view (that the blood of Christ was shed enabling the Father to accept you and forgive you) is essential to understanding and accepting yourself.

- Because God loves you, you can love yourself.

- Because God cares about you, you must care about yourself.

- Because God has forgiven you, you must forgive yourself.

- Because God has accepted you, you must learn to accept yourself.

One of the reasons why people face an identity crisis today is that they have never gained God's perspective. Therefore, they do one of two things to compensate for their uncertainty. Either they depreciate their own worth because of feelings of inadequacy; or, on the other hand, they magnify themselves to a point of distortion, trying to prove to themselves and everybody else how important they are. Their behavior is the result of overcompensation for their lack of security in Christ.

Perhaps the diagram that follows on the next page will help you better understand this concept:

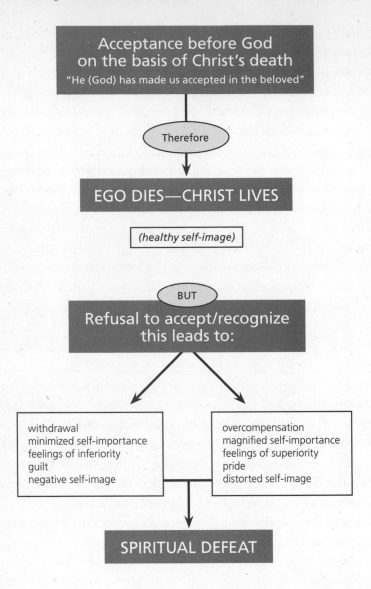

When You Minimize God's Opinion of Yourself

Until you come to grips with the fact that God completely accepts you because of what Christ did, you will never fully accept yourself. If you refuse to believe or accept the fact that God has received you, your self-image will be affected. When you minimize your importance in His eyes, five things happen:

1. You depreciate your value and worth before God. The apostle Paul wrote to the Romans, "By the grace given me I say to every one of you: Do not think of yourself more highly than you ought" (Romans 12:3). If Paul says it is wrong to have too high an opinion of yourself, is it not just as wrong to have too low an opinion of yourself?

One of the most thrilling things about Jesus is that He takes somebody who is nothing and then adds Himself, making a person of infinite value and worth. When you are a Christian and suffer from feelings of worthlessness, remember that when you take nothing and add Jesus to it, you don't end up with nothing. You end up with a vessel of clay filled with the very presence and power of God. Writing to the Corinthians, Paul likened the indwelling presence of Christ in our lives to a treasure contained in an earthen vessel. The image that would immediately have come to their minds would have been a clay pot—probably about 30 inches in height, bought in the market very cheaply. Today the equivalent of a clay pot would be a plastic bucket, something you will find in every open market in the world.

Let's say you go to Costco and purchase laundry detergent that comes in a five-gallon bucket. You are going on a trip, and you have a beautiful diamond ring that once belonged to your mother. You want to hide it for safekeeping. You think, *Nobody would ever think of looking in the detergent in the laundry room!* So you take the diamond ring and thrust it deep into the detergent. Now how much is that plastic bucket worth? Suddenly its aggregate value and worth have skyrocketed!

Getting the picture? When Christ adds Himself to the most insignificant individual, you become a person of great value. Redeemed by the blood of Jesus Christ, you're now a person of real value.

2. A negative self-image results. Symptoms are self-pity, depression, and feelings off inadequacy, worthlessness, and inferiority. You become extremely critical of yourself and begin to withdraw from people. You are sure you can't perform as well as others and tend to not try. You see yourself as very plain or just homely. You think you aren't intelligent enough to move up the ladder of promotion—and in time your conduct matches the negative image in your thinking.

I have known men and women who have gone through life defeated and downcast because they considered themselves to be of no real value. Some have been graduates of Christian universities who refused to teach a Sunday school class or even usher during a church service because of hang-ups over the past. *Not good enough,* they think.

There are times when families contribute to this problem rather than help alleviate it. Take, for instance, the young woman who wrote the following:

> I am twenty-seven years old. This is hard to admit, but I need help. I was conceived out of wedlock, which forced my mother into an early marriage at the age of 16. I definitely was not wanted and have always known it because my home was violent. This has made me feel unwanted in all situations. After my brother died, I went through a suicidal crisis...As a result, I was disfellowshipped from the church. My question is this. Can I come to God and have fellowship with Him? I did sin terribly in wanting to commit suicide, and I didn't come into the world in God's perfect will so I find it very difficult to believe. Please answer my letter because I am hurting on the inside.

Who wouldn't hurt, having grown up with a home situation such as this? When you tend to struggle with feelings of inferiority, ask yourself, *Are these feelings from God?* Of course, your answer is in the negative. C.S. Lewis once wrote that you sometimes have to tell your feelings where to get off. He explained that when he was an atheist, there were times when Christianity looked very probable, and since he had become a believer, there had been times when atheism had looked quite probable as well. Without emotional stability, he contended, you dither back and forth, driven by whims of emotion and never sure of yourself.

Regardless of your feelings, you must remind yourself that you are a person of value in God's sight. And another thought before moving ahead. No one can make you feel inferior unless you allow him to do so. So don't give the person permission to make you feel less valuable than how God sees you. Cling to what you know—you are a person of value and worth!

3. You are buffeted by unmerited guilt. Another characteristic of the individual who minimizes the importance of self is constant harassment by guilt feelings. Sarah was like that. I met her for the first time when I was asked to visit her two-month-old infant, who had been born with five tiny holes in her heart. Doctors had told the parents that the tiny holes would enlarge as the baby grew older and that nothing could be done. Her life expectancy would be about two years, and that would be punctuated by suffering and constant medical attention.

At the children's hospital I donned a white gown and mask to enter the room where the little baby lay. As I stood up by the side of the crib and looked down into the face of that innocent little girl, the mother turned to me and with tears in her eyes blurted out, "Why is God punishing my baby for what I have done?"

As we walked the hospital corridor together, Sarah began telling how she had grown up in a home with little love. Her parents were strict disciplinarians who would tell her, "God will get you if you are bad." Her concept of God was that of a cosmic policeman in hobnail boots who would grind you into the asphalt when you were bad.

At the age of 16, Sarah decided to have her "fun" no matter what God did to her, and for a period of time she lived a careless life. Then a couple of years later as she walked down the street, she heard music drifting out of the open windows of a church. She hesitated and then slipped into the building where she heard a simple message of God's love and forgiveness. She went forward and prayed to receive Christ as her personal Savior, although not understanding the nature of God's forgiveness.

After she married, a series of disasters befell the new young couple. Each time something happened, Sarah was certain that God was punishing her for what she had done before she became a Christian. A flood devastated their little home and completely destroyed all their possessions. The first child born to the couple was stillborn, and now this little baby had been born with five tiny holes in her heart.

Was God punishing her child for what she had done? No, of course not! "If anyone is in Christ, he is a new creation; the old has gone, the new has come!" (2 Corinthians 5:17)—but Sarah didn't realize that. The continued guilt she felt was just as real as though God had directly been wreaking His vengeance upon her family.

That night I prayed, "Oh, God, please let this child live so this mother will know that when You forgive us, You wipe the slate clean as though we had never sinned." In time, that mother came to accept the fact that God had forgiven her and that the problem with her child wasn't punishment for the sins that Christ had long since forgiven.

That child, not expected to live beyond the age of two, was a very normal, healthy teenager at my last contact, and the five tiny holes in her heart had knit together—nothing short of a miracle!

However, what happens when you cannot accept yourself as a person of value and worth in the sight of God?

4. Personal appearance often becomes neglected. A negative self-image causes you to reason, "Since I'm not any good anyway, why should I be concerned about my weight or how I look?" Soon you have neglected yourself and are carrying around an extra 30 pounds of not-so-beautiful weight. You don't bother to keep your hair and nails groomed properly. You not only suffer from feelings of negative self-image, you rapidly become inferior. You become inferior because you *think* you are!

When you realize the worth you have in the sight of God, there is reason to recognize that your body has become the literal dwelling place of God, the Holy Spirit. "Do you not know that your body is a temple of the Holy Spirit, who is in you?" wrote Paul to the Corinthians. He continued, "You are not your own; you were bought with a price" (1 Corinthians 6:19-20). Acknowledging that the price was paid at Calvary gives incentive to prove yourself the person of value and worth that you really are.

After my wife spoke to a women's group about self-acceptance in a biblical context, a woman came to her and said, "Every morning I look in the mirror and say to myself, 'You are really ugly!' But I will never do that again!" She understood what her real value was!

5. You never feel good enough to merit God's love or acceptance. One of the saddest letters I have received in well over four decades of broadcasting came from a woman who was then in her seventies. She asked the question, "How good must you be for God to love you?" and told the story of her life.

Had she been conceived today, it is unlikely that she would have lived to full term. She probably would have been a casualty—one of millions of babies whose lives are snuffed out by an abortionist. In her case, however, her mother gave her away at birth and she ended up in an orphanage. On Sundays, she explained, the boys and girls were lined up like animals in a dog show and prospective adopting parents came to look them over.

Since she was told by orphanage personnel, "You must be very good if you are ever going to be adopted," being left behind made her feel completely inferior. At the age of 12, however, she was adopted. She still felt that the love of her adopting parents was earned based on how good she was. At the age of 16, a friend invited her to church where, for the first time in her life, she heard that God loved her and had sent His Son to be her Savior. This was the best news she had ever heard, and that evening she responded to the invitation. When she got home, however, she knelt by the side of her bed and prayed that God would let her die that night because she was afraid she could never be "good enough" for Him to love her back.

She then asked, "Does God perform plastic surgery of the heart, erasing the trauma of our childhood?" Actually, Jesus is a specialist at healing broken hearts and removing the emotional scars that have been inflicted by cruel perpetrators of hatred.

6. Your potential is diminished. Two individuals apply for a position with a growing company. One is positive, secure, and confident; the other is hesitant, tentative, and uncertain. Who gets the job? The one who knows where he is going in life.

No wonder major corporations spend millions of dollars utilizing the services of motivational speakers who challenge employees to reach beyond themselves and stretch their potential. Does it work? The fact that companies invest so extensively speaks for itself.

Attitude is everything. It becomes a self-fulfilling prophecy, and your understanding of who you are—your self-image—becomes a barometer of your success in life. Ethel Waters, whose beautiful voice mesmerized a generation that not only appreciated her music but admired how she had risen from poverty and obscurity, put it so positively when she said, "God don't back no flops!"

In this section, I've discussed characteristics of a negative self-image—the person who sees himself or herself as less than he or she really is. Now, let's take a look at the characteristics of the person who distorts his self-worth because he hasn't found the liberating truth that he can be himself and nothing more because God accepts him on the basis of what Christ has done.

When You Overcompensate

1. You have an inflated opinion of your own self-worth. Such was the businessman who arrived at the gate too late to claim his seat and was asked to take a later flight. Walking up to the ticket agent behind the counter, he explained that he had been "bumped" from the flight. Then striving to look as important as possible asked, "Do you know who I am?" The agent squinted at the man, then picked up the mike for the PA system and announced, "There's a man here at the gate who doesn't know who he is. If anybody here can identify him, please step forward." Perfect squelch!

When you really understand that God will accept you on the basis of what Christ did, you don't have to prove to the world how important you really are. You can take a deep breath and just be yourself, which is a great feeling! You don't have to be a put-on or a sham! Christ lives in you, so ego is pushed aside. Someone has said that "*Ego* is Edging God Out." Understanding that Christ lives in you allows you to be genuine, authentic, and real!

But the man or woman suffering from a lack of self-acceptance doesn't know that this can take place. So he or she has to let you know how important he or she really is. This person actually considers himself or herself to be indispensable. The reality is that this person is very expendable. Friends tend to humor the person or disregard his or her grandiose, "how-great-I-am" statements. Actually life goes on pretty much the same whether or not that person is present, but sometimes things run a good deal smoother when that person is absent!

2. Status is very important. When you struggle with your identity because you do not realize God accepts you as you are, you want people to know that you have taken your place in society. You tend to flash your jewelry or show off name-brand clothes or watches in such a way that people can't help noticing. Your image and status are very important. You want to be served, not serve others. You want people to know that you have an important pedigree, have been to the right schools (if they can't see that large class ring, you'll tell them anyway!), and have a very prestigious circle of friends.

The kind of a car you drive, the labels in your clothes, and even the brand of watch you wear have to convey the message "I'm better than you!"—or at least "I'm very, very good!"

I think of a young man who felt much like this. He was driving down the interstate when a truck got too close to him and sideswiped the side of his new sports car. When the vehicles stopped, he was moaning, "Look at what you did to the side of my BMW!"

"Forget your BMW," said the truck driver. "Look at your arm. It's mangled!" Immediately, the young man looked down and moaned, "My Rolex watch is gone, too!"

Do you have talents? Then remember that God is the one who gave you the ability to do what you are able to accomplish. On the walls of the sound stage of Unusual Films is a sign that reads, "Every good gift and every perfect gift comes down from the Father above...so why should you boast?"

> What you have been given by your heavenly Father is yours to use, not abuse.

Do you have money? Then remember that the Scripture says, "It is He who is giving you power to make wealth" (Deuteronomy 8:18 NASB). Don't forget that what you have today can be wiped out overnight with a bad business decision. If the market falls, the stock you own can be worth half as much six months—or six days—from now. What you have been given by your heavenly Father is yours to use, not abuse. You don't own it. (Hearses never have U-Haul trailers attached to them.) Your wealth is a loan, a stewardship God has entrusted to you.

People who are secure, who know who they are, don't find it necessary to let others know how much money they have, who their best friends are, or what things cost. It's not important to them.

Do you have prestige and influence? Then remember that promotion comes from neither the east nor the west. Rather, it is God who raises one up and sets another aside (Psalm 75:6-7). Pride is a vicious sin, which God denounces in no uncertain terms. Proverbs 6:16-18 lists several things that God hates. One of those is *haughty eyes*. And we have all heard the wisdom of Proverbs 16:18: "Pride goes before destruction, and a haughty spirit before a fall" (NKJV).

3. You are quick to recognize flaws in others, slow to see them in yourself. Frankly, it doesn't take a lot of talent to look at someone and see what's wrong with that person, but it is totally a different matter to look at yourself and see your own weaknesses. Thinking you are perceptive, you actually become slightly paranoid.

4. You want to be known by your association with others. Belonging to the right club, the right church, having the right friends—being *in* is very important to some people. Such individuals can usually be recognized by the fact that they drop names unnecessarily in conversation. Like, "Yesterday, I was with (anyone whose name has wide recognition) and he was telling me about..." Or you tend to let others know about the cost of vacations, or what you pay for clothes or computers (the very opposite of the individual on the other side of the spectrum who feels he or she has to let you know that the new dress was on sale, or that he got his suit at the thrift store).

5. You are arrogant and proud. During the first three years of my ministry, I served on the staff of one of the ten largest churches in the U.S., and during that period of time I was privileged to meet and spend time with a wide variety of quite high-profile Christian leaders. I learned very quickly that they fell into two categories: Most were humble, very gracious individuals who made the novice totally comfortable. They were good but they didn't brag about how good they were. The second category—much smaller in number—were the individuals who seemed to be looking for a vacancy in the Trinity. They wanted to be treated as royalty, superstars whose inflated egos made you uncomfortable. The truly great ones didn't have to brag about their accomplishments, drop names to show you how high up the ladder they were, or otherwise impress you with their degrees.

When my daughter was graduating from Vanguard University, I was asked to do the invocation. John Ashcroft, then governor of Missouri, later to become the U.S. attorney general, was the commencement speaker, and the two of us were escorted into a green room, where we spent about 20 minutes together. I admit I was a bit awed by his stature, but what I will always remember about the conversation is how he adroitly kept asking questions about what I did and what I thought about issues. No matter how I tried to turn the conversation around and get him to talk about himself, the interest he showed in me demonstrated how secure he was in who he was.

6. You end up being an extremely lonely individual. You are never certain who is a real friend—the kind who would go to the wall with you—or simply the kind who laughs when you are throwing the party but would pass by on the other side of the street if the money ran out. The flip side of this is the fact that some of the most well-liked, gregarious individuals are common, ordinary people, but they are the ones that make others comfortable in their presence and consequently have many friends.

Acceptance in a Biblical Perspective

Three principles of value. In one of her books, my wife, Darlene, points out that the value of a piece of art—say, a masterpiece in one of the great art galleries of the world—is dependent upon three things:

- Who painted the canvas?
- How many are there just like this one?
- What will someone pay for the painting?

Apply those three principles to yourself as a reflection of your value in God's sight.

First, made in the image of God, you came from the drawing board of heaven. You are not "a mistake who should not have been born," as one woman described herself. With genes and chromosomes, you were crafted by the Almighty, and when you were born He presented a masterpiece to the world.

Then you are one of a kind—an original without duplication. Of all the other 6.9 billion people on Planet Earth, none is a clone of you. Even if you are an identical twin, no one else feels what you feel, thinks precisely what you think, sees through your eyes, or hears with your ears.

Finally, the price that was paid for you alone demonstrates your value. John R.W. Stott, in an article in *Christianity Today,* answered the question "Am I supposed to love myself or hate myself?" He says, "A satisfactory answer cannot be given *without reference to the Cross.*" He continues, "The cross of Christ supplies the answer, for it calls us both to self-denial and to self-affirmation" (which he points out is not the same as self-love). Says Stott, "It is only when we look at the cross that we see the true worth of human beings."[1]

The cross showed your true value. Paul put it like this: "God made him who had no sin to be sin for us, so that in him we might become the righteousness of God" (2 Corinthians 5:21).

Therefore, you don't have to constantly fight feelings of inferiority and inadequacy, which produce a sense of guilt and a troubled conscience. Neither do you have to try to show how good you are through associations, possessions, or beauty or strength.

That God should have a personal interest in each of us as individuals is a tremendous thought! Here is the great big universe—so large that it defies human comprehension. Yet in the midst of it, God is interested in me as a person. Augustine, the fifth-century bishop of Hippo, said, "God loves each of us as though there were only one of us."

What does self-acceptance mean to a Christian? First, God gives to each of us who knows Christ certain spiritual gifts that enrich our lives. Paul wrote to the Corinthians that the manifestation or the outworking of the Holy Spirit is given to each believer for his profit (1 Corinthians 12:7). Then he began to enumerate the gifts, saying that God has given to each of us certain gifts that equip us for His work—which is one reason you should never underestimate the scope of your influence.

Your life touches a circle of friends. No matter how limited you think your influence may be—for good or evil—you touch lives that nobody else can influence in quite the same way and manner that you do.

Self-acceptance means, secondly, that you understand God is at work in your life. "Please be patient with me. God isn't finished with me yet!" became a popular phrase some years back. We need to keep the truth of that in mind.

Two words make all the difference in our perspective. Those words are *because* and *becoming.* When you use the word *because,* you blame God. "I am this way because" mirrors hostility. When you realize that God is at work in your life, using the circumstances to mold and shape your life, you realize that you are in the process of *becoming* the person He wants you to be. You have a hope and a future.

What the Bible calls *sanctification* is really part of the Holy Spirit's ministry in your life as God chips away at your rough edges and brings you into conformity with His will and purpose for your life.

When you can accept yourself as a person of worth and value, you can then accept adverse circumstances in life and realize that God has not forsaken you nor is He punishing you, but rather He is still guiding in the affairs of your life and home no matter what happens. You gain the assurance that you are not adrift on the ocean of life without chart or compass—instead, you are becoming the person He determined you should be long, long ago.

What happens when your baby is rushed to the hospital with a high fever and an infection that is consuming her energy and even her life? You can wring your hands and cry, "Why my baby? Why are you picking on me, God?" Or you can fall back on the assurance that you belong to Him and since you are adopted into His family, you can run to your heavenly Father and cry out, "Lord, it's me, and I really need Your help *right now!*"

The results of self-acceptance. Self-acceptance in a biblical context produces *strength in the storm.* You don't consider difficulty to be punishment because you know your sins have been dealt with and you are God's child. This is not to rule out the truth that God does discipline His children in love (see Hebrews 12:3-15), but it does focus on the fact that God "works out everything in conformity with the purpose of his will" (Ephesians 1:11).

Self-acceptance in the context of Christian faith results, second, in *an inner radiance* that comes from the indwelling presence of Christ. An inner tranquility and peace, a measure of security, result from being in touch with the divine and knowing He is fully in control of the circumstances. Peter, especially, stresses the fact that we are to focus on the beauty that results from His presence within, rather than simply being concerned with appearance, clothes, and makeup (1 Peter 3:3-6).

A third thing self-acceptance does in a Christian context is produce a *different value system,* one that puts emphasis on character, integrity, and spiritual values. When you spend large sums of money for an automobile when a smaller one would be just as satisfactory, and then say, "I can't afford to give to God's work," you are really saying, "My value system puts a much higher premium on a large car than on giving to God's work."

When you say, "I have no time to spend with my family," you are really saying, "Making money in the business is more important than my wife and children." "I don't have time to go to church" is another way of saying, "I consider a day of leisure more important than worshipping God."

From God's point of view, a regenerated value system is always a reflection of security and self-acceptance. A Christian's perspective views life as a cooperation of the human and the divine. "We are God's workmanship," wrote Paul to the Ephesians, "created in Christ Jesus to do good works" (Ephesians 2:10).

Finally, self-acceptance and a joyous, radiant life go hand in hand. They aren't synonymous but they complement each other.

Who are you? Understanding who you really are enables you to boldly say,

- "I'm a person of great value and worth."
- "I'm a person whom Jesus loves, so I can love myself."
- "I'm a person who is becoming the person God wants me to be."
- "I'm just me and I wouldn't want to be anybody else in all the world!"

When you feel your self-image is slipping and you begin to forget who you are, lift your head and look up! It's important to know you are the child of a King and be proud of it. This is the way to develop healthy emotions and become all that God intends you to be.

QUESTIONS FOR THOUGHT AND DISCUSSION

John grew up in a broken home—his father had left when John was two years old. Since he was the fifth child, he wore hand-me-down clothes and had to fight for attention. He later put himself through college by waiting tables at two restaurants. Now, as an adult, he constantly puts other people down, brags about his influential contacts, and refuses to listen to criticism at work.

1. John seems very confident of himself and his life. How might his behavior be seen as a cover-up for feelings of insecurity?

2. What is one area in your life for which you used to either minimize or overcompensate but no longer do? How did that change happen?

3. Appearance, performance, and influence are three things people use to try to impress others. What is one thing in each of these categories that you are sometimes tempted to use to impress others? How is that connected to areas of

insecurity, and what steps can you take to stop your pattern of overcompensating?

4. Name one thing that you do not like about yourself. As you see it, what is one way this characteristic has a negative effect on your life? Name three ways this can be a positive thing for you. If you have trouble seeing it as a positive thing, think about someone you know who has the same defect—whether or not to the same degree as you—who does not seem troubled by it. What are three ways that person might say the characteristic positively impacts his life?

This Will Hurt...

When you feel like you have something to prove, whether to yourself or to other people, it will hurt to react automatically, following the course of habit. It will hurt to belittle another person or step in to show how much more competent you are.

This Will Help...

Learn to identify that puffed-up feeling for what it is—an insecurity. Look for ways you can redirect your thinking. Ask a trusted friend to help you begin to see those things as insecurities.

It will help to take a look at people you know who are very secure. Cultivate in your own life the qualities you see in them.

CHAPTER 3

Making Your Emotions
Work for You

"Why did you do that?" is a question that parents have asked from the days of Adam and Eve to the present. Softening the bluntness of the question, I have, on occasion, asked a wayward husband or wife, "Would you mind telling me what led you to do what you have done?" Amazingly, whether it is a six-year-old kid who took a knife and carved his initials on a piece of furniture or a husband who wounded his wife's heart by carrying on an affair with his secretary, thinking that one time wouldn't matter, the answers are very much the same.

"I felt like it" is often the first response I hear. While I've never said this, I have been tempted to ask, "Had your brain gone out your ear for a drink of water and not come back?" I mean, "How could you have gambled happiness, your relationship with your wife and family, and—God knows—your integrity, for thirty minutes of illicit passion?"

"You felt like it!" Of course, just as David did when, from his rooftop, he saw a beautiful woman bathing. "Did you, even for a moment, think of the consequences of what your passion would produce? The inevitable certainty that sooner or later the sunlight would shine on your actions and bring darkness to a relationship that you really value?"

Yes, feelings are powerful. Associated with emotions that are divorced from logic or reason, they can take you places that angels fear to tread. Alternatively, feelings can motivate you to altruistic heights you never thought possible.

Defining Emotions

Emotions are what lies behind your feelings, so let's strive to define them—which, I have discovered, is somewhat like nailing Jell-O to the wall. Of course, everybody knows what emotions are—until we strive to agree on a definition.

"Emotions," says James Drever's *Dictionary of Psychology,* "are a state of excitement or perturbation, marked by strong feelings and usually an impulse towards a definite form of behavior."[1]

A more contemporary definition contends,

> An emotion is a mental and psychological state associated with a wide variety of feelings, thoughts, and behaviors. It is a prime determinant of the sense of subjective well-being and appears to play a central role in many human activities. As a result of this generality, the subject has been explored in many if not all of the human sciences and art forms. There is much controversy concerning how emotions are defined and classified.[2]

The *Merriam-Webster* dictionary says this: "a departure from the normal calm state to strong feelings, an impulse toward actions." Some psychologists believe that emotions and feelings operate as separate entities, yet for practical purposes feelings stem from emotions and are an extension of them, motivating people in one direction or another. If you are part of a growing minority of people who struggled through a few years of Latin at one time or another, you may remember that the English word *emotion* is derived from the Latin verb *emovere,* meaning "to remove."

But you don't need a definition! You know what they are, and you have a pretty good idea of what they do—both negatively and positively. Emotions are to life what pigment is to paint; they make life bright and beautiful, or dark and dreary. They put the sparkle in the eyes of the young woman who has responded to the love of a suitor, and they can slowly close the blinds of joy on the aged grandfather whose wife of many years has expired, as a gloomy cloud of depression descends upon him.

Someone once said that you should always study history in the morning because in the afternoon there is more history to study. While I have no intention of boring you with a lengthy history of emotions and how they are expressed, I have to say that from the day Moses chose to chronicle the exploits of our first parents, Adam and Eve, to the present, the vast landscape of history has been painted with emotions that have remained very much unchanged over the centuries.

The ancient Greek Stoics were among the first to strive to organize and understand emotions. Both Plato and Aristotle added their two cents' worth, and then in more modern days René Descartes, Baruch Spinoza, and David Hume explored them. William James (1842–1910) was a pioneer in modern research. The son of a theologian who trained as a medical doctor, he grew up in a Christian home. He

> We humans came from the drawing board of heaven with emotions on board, ready to paint the landscape of life.

rubbed shoulders with the intellectual elite of the nineteenth century and developed theories about emotions that laid the foundation for modern studies.

A casual study of the theory of emotions and how they are classified, however, reveals one truth: There is little agreement on what emotions are, how many there are, and how you classify them.

At the risk of stating the obvious, though, may I remind you that we humans came from the drawing board of heaven with emotions on board, ready to paint the landscape of life. They were no evolutionary development, as followers of Darwin have postulated. Read the account of Moses, its events now 3500 years in the past, and you find passion, hatred, murder, and love—all motivating people to do something that, at times, bore no relationship whatsoever to logic or a sense of rightness.

We Were Created as Emotional Beings

Emotions are part of your being. They are not something to be suppressed but something to be understood, appreciated, and allowed to lift you to higher realms and experiences. They should not depress you, darken your life, or send you into chaos! Repress or remove emotions from your life, and the landscape becomes sterile, barren, desolate, and cold.

No matter how you may count or classify the gamut of human emotions, there is something that needs to be recognized. You have emotions, and feelings which emanate from them, because you were made in the image of God.

"So does God have emotions?" you ask. Though this may be something you have never thought much about, the Bible says that God's emotions, with few exceptions, are much the same as the ones that color your life. A study of God's emotions reveals much about his nature and character. Consider the following:

- *God loves!* No stronger proof text can be summoned than one of the most often quoted texts, John 3:16: "God so loved the world that he gave his one and only Son." What can be clearer than these words: "Whoever does not love does not know God, because God is love" (1 John 4:8)? The Swiss theologian Karl Barth was once asked what was the greatest theological truth he had ever discovered, and he is reported to have responded, "Jesus loves me, this I know, for the Bible tells me so."

- *God also hates those things that destroy what He loves.* "'I hate divorce,' says the LORD God of Israel, 'and I hate a man's covering himself with violence as well as with his garment,' says the LORD Almighty. So guard yourself in your spirit, and do not break faith" (Malachi 2:16).

  "There are six things the Lord hates," says Proverbs 6:16,

followed by "seven that are detestable to him." The writer then lists them: "haughty eyes, a lying tongue, hands that shed innocent blood, a heart that devises wicked schemes, feet that are quick to rush into evil, a false witness who pours out lies and a man who stirs up dissension among brothers."

- *God can be grieved,* contended Paul as he wrote to the Ephesians, saying, "Do not grieve the Holy Spirit of God, with whom you were sealed for the day of redemption" (Ephesians 4:30).

- *God, on occasion, is also angry.* While I will develop this thought more fully in the chapter on anger, I want to point out that God's wrath (strong anger) targets those who stand in opposition to His purpose and will. Says Paul, "God's wrath comes on those who are disobedient" (Ephesians 5:6). John, writing of the judgment of God upon a world who has rejected His Son, writes of "the winepress of God's wrath" (Revelation 14:19).

Emotions Add Color to Life's Landscape

What would music, art, poetry, or literature be without emotion? Can you fathom how George Frideric Handel's *Messiah* would sound, were there no emotional triggers that move your heart as you hear the refrain, "And He shall reign forever and ever," as well as the magnificent crescendo, "Hallelujah! Hallelujah, Hallelujah!"

Great artists know the power of emotions as they paint life in terms that universally speak to our hearts. William Shakespeare, whose writings are often considered second in importance only to the Bible in the English-speaking world, was a master when it came to conveying emotional responses. Remember these often quoted lines from *Macbeth*? "Will all great Neptune's ocean wash this blood clean from my hand? No, this my hand will rather the multitudinous seas incarnadine, making the green one red."[3]

Ignacy Paderewski, the great Polish pianist and, incidentally, the first prime mister of modern Poland, was a person of great emotional sensitivity.

It is said that when the great maestro was scheduled to play a concert in a building, he would go to that place several hours before the concert was to begin and sit quietly soaking up the ambience of the facility so that the room would become a part of himself, and so once the concert had begun, there would be nothing about the building that would distract him or bottle up the flow of music that came from his innermost being.

Fritz Kreisler, the great violinist, once made arrangements to meet a friend when he was en route to a concert. When the train stopped at his friend's town, Kreisler tucked his precious violin under his arm and eagerly disembarked to find his friend. When it came time to board the train again, Kreisler began searching for his ticket. To his chagrin, it was nowhere to be found. He tried to convince the ticket collector that he really was Fritz Kreisler and that he had forgotten his ticket, leaving it on the train.

The skeptical agent eyed the violin under his arm and then replied, ✐ "If you really are Fritz Kreisler, then let me hear you play your violin, because nobody in the world can play like Fritz Kreisler." There on the train platform, Kreisler opened his well-worn violin case and played for the skeptical but pleased ticket agent.

What was it that made Kreisler's playing so distinct that even an amateur musician would know the difference? His brilliant emotional sensitivity!

Emotions Are the Prime Movers of People

On November 19, 1863, President Abraham Lincoln spoke at Gettysburg. His words were simple, powerful, and laden with emotion. Who could have thought so few words could have so moved so many people, as he began, "Fourscore and seven years ago our fathers brought forth on this continent a new nation, conceived in liberty, and dedicated to the proposition that all men are created equal." He closed with the words, "We here highly resolve that these dead shall not have died in vain, that this nation, under God, shall have a new birth of freedom, and that government of the people, by the people, for the people, shall not perish from the earth."

Maligned by some but revered by many, this man moved people's emotions. His words spoke to the hearts of men and women whose lives

had been torn to shreds by the carnage of one of history's bloodiest battles. His words now stand immortal.

Now fast-forward 77 years.

It was the spring of 1940; Britain was taking heavy losses at the hands of the Germans. On May 26, the evacuation from Dunkirk began. On June 4, Winston Churchill went before the House of Commons and brought one of the most challenging and emotion-fraught messages ever delivered. He closed with these words:

> We shall go on to the end, we shall fight in France, we shall fight on the seas and oceans, we shall fight with growing confidence and growing strength in the air, we shall defend our Island, whatever the cost may be, we shall fight on the beaches, we shall fight on the landing grounds, we shall fight in the fields and in the streets, we shall fight in the hills; we shall never surrender, and even if, which I do not for a moment believe, this Island or a large part of it were subjugated and starving, then our Empire beyond the seas, armed and guarded by the British Fleet, would carry on the struggle, until, in God's good time, the New World, with all its power and might, steps forth to the rescue and the liberation of the old.

What would have been the impact of the words of Winston Churchill in World War 2 had they not been impregnated with emotion? This great orator inspired and moved the very soul of the British people during the difficult war years. When the bombs were falling and a German invasion seemed imminent, Churchill's words marshaled reserves of steel as he concluded, "Let us therefore brace ourselves to our duties, and so bear ourselves that if the British Empire and its Commonwealth last for a thousand years, men will still say, 'This was their finest hour.'"

Across the cold English Channel the mad Fuhrer also moved people with emotions. His fiery rhetoric inspired the cheering masses, who quickly became mesmerized by his forceful words.

No orator, artist, minister, writer, or poet has ever succeeded in his profession without the ability to use emotion in such a way that the lives of people are deeply touched.

The Welsh revival, which shook that little country for God about the turn of the twentieth century, was triggered by the words of a teenage girl who stood up in a midweek prayer meeting and forcefully said, "I do love Jesus..." Then she began sobbing as she repeated the words. Unable to maintain her composure, she sat down and continued weeping softly. The deeply stirred feelings of her heart, fed by the fervent prayers of God's people, began to spread, and revival broke out.

Was Jesus Emotional?

Says psychologist Dr. Bruce Narramore,

> The Bible describes more than 20 different emotions that Jesus felt. And they weren't all happy feelings, either! Among others, Jesus felt affection, anguish, anger, compassion, distress, grief, gladness, indignation, joy, love, peace, sadness, sympathy, troubled and weary. If Christ is our model of perfect spiritual and emotional maturity, perhaps we can learn by taking a look at a few of Jesus' emotions![4]

On at least two occasions He wept openly—something we often think "real men" don't do. Consider these words, "When Jesus landed and saw a large crowd, he had compassion on them and healed their sick" (Matthew 14:14). Compassion, the very opposite of indifference, means you feel what another person feels. You hurt where they hurt. You relate to what they experience. You cry with them.

Then do you recall how Jesus wept at the tomb of His friend Lazarus? And then He cried over His beloved Jerusalem, saying, "O Jerusalem, Jerusalem, you who kill the prophets and stone those sent to you, how often I have longed to gather your children together, as a hen gathers her chicks under her wings, but you were not willing!" (Luke 13:34).

There is far more behind the story of Lazarus than you observe in a simple reading. Twice the text of John stresses the fact that Jesus loved Lazarus. The sisters instruct the servant who finds Jesus to say, "Lord, the one you love is sick." And then John adds these words after Jesus responds to their entreaty, "Jesus loved Martha and her sister and Lazarus" (John

11:3,5). No wonder He cried openly and unashamedly as He stood before the sealed tomb. He cared. No, He wasn't sorrowful for his friend Lazarus; He knew that death had not permanently claimed him. He wept because He cared for Mary and Martha and joined in their grief.

Although there is no record of Jesus' ever being moved to laughter, I am convinced that He did laugh, not with the ribald laughter produced by the garrulous emptiness of many today—but with a sense of humor that originated deep within His heart. Laughter is joy bubbling from the heart, and when John describes Him as "full of joy" you can be sure that on occasion His joy bubbled over with laughter.

Jesus empathized with people in their deepest needs, thereby showing us that the display of emotions is not a sign of weakness. Emotions are the manifestations of your heart. It is this that makes you human—not a robot which moves on command or impulse to do the bidding of a controlling power.

Starter Emotions—Love, Fear, Anger

Though psychologists debate which emotions an infant is born with, when a child comes into the world kicking and screaming, voicing pleasure or displeasure over having been delivered from the security of a mother's womb, it is absolutely certain that an emotional being has taken his place in the world and is able and willing to let you know how he or she feels. When the child is hungry, nonverbal communication kicks into high gear as he wails the message, "I want to be fed!"

Hold an infant loosely in your arms and the child immediately expresses fear of falling, but cradle the baby securely in your arms and he or she quickly relaxes. Months before a child is born that infant recognizes the voice of its mother and responds to her gentle comfort and soothing.

The facial patterns of infants—smiles, frowns, knit brows, tears, and puckered mouths—are far more reliable barometers of emotions than those of poker-faced adults who have been programmed not to show emotions, or who think that displaying feelings is inappropriate.

As an infant grows into a child, a plethora of emotional responses colors his life: disgust, shame, tenderness, awe, reverence, joy, grief, jealousy, pride,

greed, hatred, ecstasy, remorse, excitement, envy, worry, and happiness—
to name but a few.

There are times when more than one emotion sways you at the same
time. Have you ever heard of a love-hate relationship? Sometimes emotions
that seem to be opposites are both present. Ambivalence, as psychologists
describe it, occurs when you feel two opposing emotions at the same time,
each pulling you a different way.

It is perfectly normal that on occasion you feel opposing emotions
toward people you really care about. You'll feel that way when you discover your four year old has written, "I LOVE YOU, MOMMY!" on the
wall with your lipstick. You'll feel that way when your youngster brings
in a bouquet of flowers for you, ones that he picked himself—from your
neighbor's garden.

A newspaper article told of a man whose tiny boat overturned in the
South China Sea. He later told reporters that he was happy, but fearful
at the same time—happy because it was the first time in two months
that his wife clung to him, but fearful because he couldn't swim and the
waters were full of sharks.

There are emotions that compete for dominance, with each voicing its
own particular merits, creating a situation that is confusing—a kind of
emotional schizophrenia—forcing you to decide which of two opposite
courses of action to take. Should you rein in your desire for "forbidden
fruit"? Or do you yield to your passion, justifying it by telling yourself,
*God made me and gave me these wonderful impulses and emotions, so can
it be wrong for me to indulge them?*

That's when your value system and your core religious beliefs kick into
operation and direct your conscience to approve or disapprove what your
emotions are prompting you to do. Moral choices and decisions trigger
emotional responses that can produce guilt and shame or contentment
and fulfillment.

Again it is because you were made in God's image that you make judg-
ments that lower forms of animals are not troubled with. Subsequently,
when you deny God the opportunity to invade your value system, you
can end up doing all sorts of things that would trouble the consciences
of other people.

In 1969, an incident that took place in Vietnam outraged the world. Led by Lieutenant William Calley Jr., American soldiers attacked and killed more than 300 civilians in the village of My Lai. This incident became known as the My Lai Massacre. The world was shocked by the brutality and callous murders of unarmed, helpless civilians, including women and children.

When the facts of the situation finally became known, Calley defended his actions, saying that his conscience had prompted him to order the military action to avenge the death of a buddy who had been killed by the Vietcong. And the man who finally blew the whistle on the whole sordid event did so because *his conscience* was troubled by the whole ordeal, which he believed to be wrong—criminally wrong.

Is your conscience to be trusted? That depends upon the values you hold dear to your heart and what you believe to be right or wrong. The Ten Commandments still carry force in God's perspective! You can be relatively certain that the emotions that are prompted by your conscience are right and proper if biblical principles have molded your conscience— principles such as the belief that all people are of value in the sight of God; that there are certain actions that are right or wrong; that you have no right to another's wife, property, or employees; that some things are moral and others are immoral; and that truth and falsehood are clearly defined.

Don't forget that in recent years a genre of terrorists has come into existence who not only lay down their lives for a cause they believe in but strive to take as many other lives as possible in their quest for destruction. A misaligned conscience prompts them to do what others detest and believe to be not only wrong morally but despicably criminal.

Emotions and Your Physical Body

God created you as a composite of three elements—distinct yet indivisible and inseparable—the emotional, the physical, and the spiritual. You cannot submit to an X-ray or MRI scan and sort out the various components that make you a person, though we would often like to do so.

I compare the relationship of these three to a cylinder filled with liquid, with wire mesh separating three sections. Punch a hole in the side of the cylinder and the contents all drain to the same level. And that illustrates how your emotions, as well as your physical body along with your spiritual life, all take hits when you encounter difficulty.

First, let's consider how emotions affect your health and your physical body. All competent medical authorities are quick to recognize the relationship between your emotions and your physical well-being. In his book *None of These Diseases,* Dr. S.I. McMillen (a medical doctor) asks the question, "Is it not a remarkable fact that our *reactions* to stress determine whether stress is going to cure us or make us sick?"[5] He says your attitude determines whether emotions will make you *better* or *bitter.*

Positive emotions add vitality to life. How you view the circumstances of your life—whether you are an optimist or an inveterate pessimist—may even make the difference between life and death in extremely difficult situations. This fact was borne out by the experiences of prisoners of war in the concentration camps of Europe in World War 2.

In September of 1942, a young doctor, his new bride, and his mother, father, and brother were arrested and taken to a concentration camp in Bohemia. Known as prisoner number 119,104, Victor Frankl slowly saw his life unravel. But as a psychiatrist, Frankl viewed life within the camp through different eyes. He observed that some survived and others were overwhelmed by a fatalism that snuffed out any hope.

He saw four reactions of prisoners that were experienced in varying degrees: 1) shock upon arrival; 2) apathy, becoming accustomed to restrictions and repression; 3) bitterness over having their lives and families disrupted; and 4) disillusionment—the most devastating and deadly of all.

Viktor Frankl was one of those who lived to tell about it. In his book *Man's Search for Meaning,* cited as one of the ten most influential books in America following its release in 1946, the author describes how those who gave up hope often curled up in fetal positions and died, while those who were committed to strong religious belief in some way survived.

He wrote,

> The prisoner who had lost faith in the future—his future—
> was doomed. With his loss of belief in the future, he also lost
> his spiritual hold; he let himself decline and became subject

to mental and physical decay…He simply gave up. There he remained…nothing bothered him anymore.[6]

When you are confronted with danger, your emotions trigger your adrenal system, which pumps large doses of adrenaline into your bloodstream. This enables you to perform almost superhuman feats. No doubt you have read of situations—say a car has overturned—when in the face of danger a petite woman single-handedly lifted an automobile or other very large object, allowing her to save the life of someone she loved.

When my son was about two years old, we lived in a suburban area fairly close to the woods. Reports of packs of wild dogs attacking children had caused us to exercise as much caution as possible, but no parent can keep a two year old confined to the house all the time. I was in the study when suddenly I heard the loud barking of dogs and the frantic screams of a child—my only son, Steven.

The instant the sound registered in my brain, I leaped for the door to rescue the child, not noticing that the screen was firmly latched. I burst through the door, knocking the latch off as though it was not there. As soon as the stray German shepherd saw me, the dog turned and ran. That probably saved its life—I am quite certain I would have attacked or killed that dog with my bare hands regardless of how badly mauled I might have been in the process. The life of my son was threatened, so I thought.

At the time I crashed through the door, I felt nothing, but in the days that followed my left side turned black and blue from the impact. That's the force of adrenaline triggered by an emotional response.

Negative emotions can literally destroy you physically. Emotions affect a variety of physical systems—the number of red corpuscles, the reduction of awareness of fatigue under stress, the rate of your heart, your respiration, and even your temperature.

Bitterness, hatred, envy, anger, and other negative feelings trigger harmful responses in our bodies. Helen Kooiman reports that a well-known doctor of internal medicine at the Mayo Clinic used to say, "I tell my patients they cannot afford to hold a grudge or maintain hate." The doctor "went on to give an illustration of how he saw a man kill himself, as he put it, 'inch by inch,' because of a quarrel with a sister over a family estate. The man became so embittered within himself that his breath was foul, and the organs of his body ceased to function properly, and in a matter of months he was physically dead." The man literally killed himself a day at a time.

> Psychologists believe that 60 percent of all hospital beds are filled with patients whose problems are psychosomatic in origin.

Negative emotions are the root causes of psychosomatic illnesses. The fact that something is labeled *psychosomatic* doesn't, for a moment, mean that the illness is not real. Believe me, it is very real, but it means that the physical problem—be it an ulcer, hypertension, heart trouble, or a skin rash—is triggered by an emotional response.

Psychologists believe that 60 percent of all hospital beds are filled with patients whose problems are psychosomatic in origin. Some, including Dr. Dennis Cope, believe the figure is much higher. Cope, once voted outstanding professor at the UCLA School of Medicine in Los Angeles, is an endocrinologist, a committed believer in Jesus Christ, and is active in his church. I once asked him if he believed that the percentage was that high. He thought for a moment. "Actually," he said, "I believe the figure runs much closer to 80 to 85 percent!" What a price to pay for negative emotions!

Consider the following:

- A study at Oschner Clinic in New Orleans, based on 5000 cases of gastrointestinal disorders, concluded that 74 percent of their patients' problems were emotionally induced.

- The outpatient clinic of New York University has stated that 76 percent of their patients are there because of emotional stress.

- A study at the University of Colorado's Department of Medicine indicated that the majority of their patients harbored deep-seated bitterness, grudges against someone, or resentment over something.

- A study conducted by John Schindler, MD, claims that emotions tighten the skeletal and muscular internal organs and lead to emotional arthritis. Schindler's study is available in most medical libraries.[7]

The Bible says negative emotions are to be recognized and dealt with in the appropriate manner. And when you fail to do this, you often pay the price in physical suffering. Take, for instance, the effect of hatred and bitterness. In the 1960s I first confronted this issue when I was counseling four separate individuals, all of whom were Christians—in fact two were missionaries. But all four were extremely bitter against someone or over a situation involving the mission they were serving.

Within a two-year period, all four succumbed to cancer. I began to connect the dots and saw a pattern. Subsequent research done by professionals reflects a pattern of relationship between cancer and your emotions. A study done by the University of Michigan confirms this conclusion. Dr. Michelle Riba, the director of the Psycho-Oncology Program at the same institution, says that emotional problems are almost always intertwined with the cancer that has brought someone for professional help.[8] Enter the phrase "cancer and emotions" in an Internet search and you will immediately find many articles documenting the relationship between your thinking and emotions and your physical body.

Bitterness against an individual becomes a poison—not one that destroys your enemy but one that gradually destroys you. Dr. McMillen is right when he contends that your emotions will make you better or bitter. They can kill you or give you strength to survive in the darkest of circumstances. They will be either a cause for rejoicing or a curse.

Emotions and Your Mind

Your emotions are not rigid like pieces of steel in spans of concrete; they are fluid and flexible and extremely complex, bending with your physical sensations and the impulses of the mental conditioning that affects your thinking. The Bible tells us that as a man thinks in his heart, so is he (see Proverbs 23:7 KJV). Your thinking is what gives guidance to your emotions, either negatively or positively. It contributes to the inner struggles you have, or lessens them.

Conditioning. Your emotions are conditioned not only by your belief system but also by your culture and the values of the family in which you are raised. Most introductory psychology courses review the experiments by Ivan Pavlov that demonstrate the fact that emotional responses follow the conditioning to which they have been subjected. Let me illustrate.

Perhaps you were fortunate enough to get a ticket to the opening ceremonies of the Olympics—something you will never forget. As athletes from various countries marched by, each delegation bearing the flag of their home country, you watched and, perhaps, politely clapped your hands in acknowledgment. Then…at last, the American delegation marched by, proudly waving the Stars and Stripes as the band played "The Star-Spangled Banner"! The sight of your flag deeply stirred the feelings of your heart. You couldn't help it—you choked up and a tear came to your eyes.

Why? The flag of your country is simply a piece of cloth—various colors stitched onto a backing—just like the other flags which had preceded it. The difference is what it represents—your home, your country, and your people. Everything you love is wrapped up in what it represents. It's not *just a piece of cloth*—it represents what you live for; and the sight of the American flag waving in the breeze triggers the emotional response of your heart.

Your emotions can be conditioned in such a manner that what you once felt strongly about just doesn't influence you in the same manner. In psychological warfare, it is called *brainwashing,* a term that was introduced into the English language following the Korean War, when a relatively high percentage of American GIs defected. Brainwashing included sleep deprivation, a disturbing reality (say, an electric light that was shined in your eyes 24 hours a day), and a bombardment of propaganda. Gradually the person's psychological resistance was so battered that he gradually began to believe and think what he otherwise would have rejected.

When it comes to our lives and marriages, the same thing is true, perhaps in a slightly different manner. Strong emotions such as love and faith can be battered by circumstances that gradually cause those strong impulses to subside or even die.

Emotions are flexible and can be channeled into productive areas. Why does God not let us off the hook for wrongdoing, accepting our shallow excuses that we did what we did because "we felt like it"? First, accountability before God demands that we be responsible for our choices. The uniform teaching of Scripture is that we are accountable, and therefore we can control our reactions to circumstances and situations. Don't forget, God didn't let Adam off after hearing his plea: "She [meaning Eve] took of the fruit and I did eat it." In other words, "Don't blame me; she's the one who gave it to me." (See Deuteronomy 24:16; Ezekiel 18:19-23; Romans 3:23.)

Directing your emotions. Let's go one step further. God created humans as emotional beings. If, however, an individual cannot control or direct his or her emotions (that is, an individual is not capable of keeping himself from doing what he feels pulled to do by his emotions) and yet God holds the person accountable for what he does, then God judges us unfairly!

When there is a struggle between your emotions and your will, your emotions win out only when you disregard the power of your own will, because your emotions are controlled by and are subject to your will. When you choose to let emotions control your behavior, you have, as an act of your will, decided to bypass your intellect and often your knowledge of what is right or wrong.

"But I love him—I can't help it!"

"I just don't feel like praying, so I won't be a hypocrite doing something I don't feel like doing!"

"Surely it can't be wrong, because God gave me those beautiful feelings and I was doing what came naturally!"

Statements such as these reflect the popular notion that you are not really responsible for the emotional responses of your human body. Are you subject to their whims and fancies, driven to and fro in life by their great powers? Let's look further at these powerful forces.

Either your thinking will control your emotions, or your emotions will control your thinking. The Bible says a great deal about your thinking and how what you think relates to your emotions. Consider these statements:

> Commit thy works unto the LORD, and thy thoughts shall be established (Proverbs 16:3 KJV).

> We demolish arguments and every pretension that sets itself up against the knowledge of God, and we take captive every thought to make it obedient to Christ (2 Corinthians 10:5).

The Bible instructs us to focus on positive thoughts, which in turn bring wholesome emotional responses. Paul wrote,

> Whatever is true, whatever is noble, whatever is right, whatever is pure, whatever is lovely...think about such things (Philippians 4:8).

You will never be able to fully control your environment, and you often cannot change your culture. There will always be people who rub you the wrong way. The weather won't always suit you; neighbors may not please you; but you will never be in a position in which you cannot choose your emotional response to your environment, and this knowledge is liberating.

Viktor Frankl believed that people who were imprisoned in the concentration camps of World War 2 made a fundamental decision as to whether or not they would act or react to their circumstances, and their decision had everything to do with their destiny. He says,

> In the final analysis nobody forces you to be controlled by your environment, your poverty, or the conditions of your childhood. You have a choice. You decide how you will act, whether you return evil with evil or evil with good. Nobody can keep you from loving a person no matter how unlovable he is, and no one can keep you from hating him if you allow yourself to do so. The choice is yours.[9]

A businessman who bought a newspaper from a lad on the street every evening as he left his office learned that lesson. When he took the paper, the man would always say, "Thank you, son. Thanks very much!" One day the boy asked, "How come you always say 'Thank you!'? Other people don't bother."

"I was once a newsboy myself," replied the businessman. "I know what it is to be considered as nothing, and I determined never to treat anybody like that!"

Emotions and Your Spiritual Life

A discussion of emotions and how they affect your life would be incomplete apart from at least a brief discussion of emotions and your spiritual nature. I never cease to be amazed at the way people will go to a sporting event—say basketball, football, baseball, or soccer—and yell and scream! They cheer their team and hurl epithets at their opponents—no, they are not rednecks who have had too much beer to drink, with sweat rings on their collar and grime under their fingernails. Nice people with a good education (check out the emblems on their class rings), well-respected folks who have taken their place in society, and—here is the kicker—then they go to church on Sunday, and sit there stone-faced, bored, and apathetic, devoid of any emotional expression.

How did we convince ourselves that when it comes to the God part of our lives, that we should be as emotionless and expressionless as a corpse? It wasn't God who sent that message to humankind.

Not wanting to be thought of as religious fanatics (note that a fanatic is simply someone who loves Jesus more than you do), we think that God is best worshipped with our intellect but not with any overt expression of emotions—tears, joy, celebration, laughter, or shouting (yes, just as you did at the football game).

Take time to make a brief study of how both priests and people worshipped in the tabernacle and you will find that emotional manifestations, including what I mentioned in the previous paragraph, were all part of prescribed worship. They sang and rejoiced! They lifted their hands in worship! They ascribed to the Almighty praise and glory— all of which deeply touches the emotions. In Psalm 100, worshippers were instructed to

- "shout for joy"
- "worship…with gladness"

- "come before him with joyful songs"
- "enter his gates with thanksgiving, his courts with praise"

Worship was not a spectator sport but involved all who were active participants in rejoicing in God's goodness because "the LORD is good and his love endures forever; his faithfulness continues through all generations" (Psalm 100:5).

Yes, I know we tend to look down on displays of emotion—people who lift their hands in praise, forgetting that what you care deeply about becomes your passion, and your passion is expressed through emotional outlets.

Passion for God is a driving force that embraces you—body, soul, and spirit. No, I'm not suggesting emotional outbursts that disrupt orderly worship, but intense emotional expression venting deep feelings of praise and intelligent worship.

Don't allow your emotions to shut down when you walk through the doors of a church or when you quietly wait on the Lord as you begin your day.

QUESTIONS FOR THOUGHT AND DISCUSSION

—————————∽∂————————

It is commonly believed that God made men rational and women emotional, but studies indicate that this stereotype is not backed up by research. With that in mind consider the following questions.

1. When you were a youngster, did the display of emotions or the lack of them that you saw expressed by your parents influence you?

2. Why do men feel that they are required to offer an apology for any show of tears in public? Is this really a weakness?

3. Do you recall when Jesus shed tears in public? Do you think people who witnessed that considered it to be weakness?

4. Why do we look down on any emotional responses to God's majesty and person in worship services?

This Will Hurt...

Tell your son, "Real men don't cry!" and you will convey a message that has the potential of inhibiting his emotional expression as an adult.

Repressing your emotions will gradually darken the landscape of your life.

This Will Help…

Men will sometimes say, "Tell me what you *think* about this!" while women will say, "Tell me how you *feel* about this!" Try switching the verbs. Get men to express their feelings and encourage women to express their thoughts as well as emotions.

Refuse to allow bitterness to creep into your life. Remember that you become the loser when you do this.

CHAPTER 4

Making Friends of
Your Emotions

Everybody knows that men and women are different. Their brains are wired differently, too, and the emotional responses of men and women seek different playing fields as well. It's a gross oversimplification to suggest that men are rational and women are emotional; however, it is quite easily demonstrated that your emotions—testosterone in men, estrogen and progesterone in women—bring different emotions into play. Women quite consistently demonstrate an emotional sensitivity that men don't possess, and quite often men possess a cerebral instinct that sees situations from a rational rather than emotional perspective. Neither perspective is better than the other. They are simply different, which demonstrates how a husband and wife complement each other, each bringing a unique perspective to the marriage relationship.

When Dr. Ann Kring was Associate Professor of Psychology at Vanderbilt University, research that she spearheaded led her to conclude:

> Men and women experience the same level of sadness while watching a tearjerker at the movies, but women are more likely to reach for a box of tissues...It is incorrect to make a blanket statement that women are more emotional than men. It is correct to say that women show their emotions more than men.[1]

Studies conducted at the University of New South Wales in Australia conclude that "women's memory tends to be empathetic, while men's is egocentric." Women tend to focus on what happens to others; men, on what happens to them. Women tend to recall information better; men, information that happened to them.[2]

Frankly, when it comes to expressing sympathy and compassion, women win over men hands down! The wife I'm about to describe would totally agree. You see, this middle-aged woman stepped out of the shower, and as she was toweling off she looked at herself in the floor-to-ceiling mirror on the closet door. Observing the bags under her eyes, the "love handles" around her waist, and the impact that gravity had on other parts of her anatomy, she turned to her husband and said, "Dear, just look at me and say something that will make me feel better about myself." He thought for a moment and replied, "Well, dear, there's certainly nothing wrong with your eyesight."

How do you make friends rather than enemies of your emotions? First, let's notice several steps you can take in coping with emotions.

1. Take Inventory of Your Emotions

Would you consider emotions to be a plus or a minus in your life? If you drew a line and labeled one end "emotionless" and the opposite end "extremely emotional," where are you on the spectrum? Your answer is dependent upon several factors—your DNA, your culture, your early emotional conditioning, your family or lack of one growing up, and even your education and status in life.

Some repress their emotions. They consider them to be detrimental to their development and maturity. "Real men don't cry," we have heard; and when you are told something enough times you buy into that mentality. How many times have you seen a situation when a man wept publicly and then said, "I apologize for crying"? Hey, if you burp in public, apologize; but why should we think that men ought to apologize for showing emotion over what is important to them? Jesus never apologized when He shed tears, right?

The reality is that real men have emotions and feelings, and to repress them by bottling them up inside is harmful emotionally, physically, and spiritually. God made you an emotional being, and in a sense the expression of deep emotions is like a relief valve that keeps you from building up stress and pressure until you explode. The longer you repress your emotions, especially negative emotions, the more volcanic will be their display when they finally come boiling to the surface. But because some people have grown up with the attitude

> To repress emotions that are part of your psychic makeup is… contrary to God's design and counterproductive to good health.

that emotional display is weakness—men in particular are supposed to be tough and not cry—it is difficult for them to express emotions, and the longer normal expression is denied the more devastating the consequences.

A father lost his son, who was in his early twenties. When the news of the boy's death reached the family, the boy's mother burst into tears, but the father turned ashen white, clenched his teeth, and fought back the tears. "John really took it like a man," his friends said. "Never shed a tear!"

They were right, too—that is, until the funeral. The minister concluded his remarks, and the people silently filed past the boy's casket as the organ softly played "Nearer, My God, to Thee"—when the boy's father, fists clenched, began quietly muttering under his breath: "God, I'll get even with You if it's the last thing I ever do." "God," he repeated, "I'll get even with You…" Suddenly, he realized what he was saying, and the tears gushed forth from his heart. As A.W. Tozer wrote,

> Be sure that human feelings can never be completely stifled.
> If they are forbidden their normal course, like a river they will
> cut another channel through the life and flow out to curse,
> and ruin, and destroy.[3]

The display of emotion—whether it is in times of grief or excitement—is not weakness. To repress emotions that are part of your psychic makeup is a contributing factor to mental illness. It's contrary to God's design and counterproductive to good health.

When you repress your emotions, they gradually shut down. I shall never forget the evening that Alex Melnuchuk sat at my dinner table and spoke of the years of imprisonment he had endured because of Communist repression in Ukraine. He had been in prison for only a few months, when he was required to visit an office in a tall building that had a window that allowed him to see over the grim wall that separated him from the world outside.

Alex told how he paused and with a lingering look saw people moving about, and the emotional impact of missing his family hit him like a ton of bricks. Of course, he wept, sorrowful that he couldn't see his wife, family, and friends on the outside. Then, said Alex, his emotions began to shut down, and for the next six years, he recounted that he was virtually without emotion.

Alex is not alone! Vast numbers of men do the same thing, whether it is caused by dads who reprove them as boys or by the impact of society that says, "To show emotion reflects weakness."

Others simply deny their emotions. This differs from repression in that the person who denies emotions refuses to come to grips with issues that would lead to emotional responses of any kind. But like keeping a new pair of shoes without any scuffs, you can't ignore emotions indefinitely. Eventually emotions have to come out of the box.

One gentleman, though, nearly succeeded. At the age of 80, his doctor gave him a clean bill of health and pronounced him a nearly perfect specimen. "What's the secret of your good health?" asked the doctor.

"It's this way, Doc," replied the old man. "When Sarah and I married 55 years ago, we decided that we wouldn't allow ourselves to get angry with each other, and I told her that instead of arguing with her, I'd just get my hat and take a long walk…So, you see, Doc, I've had a vigorous outdoor life now for many years!"

Some folks try to sidestep emotional issues rather than meeting them and making them work for them. When they are confronted with situations that could be emotional (family problems, talking to the boss, dividing the estate, and so on), they will live with situations for years, even with deep-seated feelings, and ignore the disposition of the problem.

Ignoring emotional feelings never contributes to the stability of a marriage or any other relationship. Feelings that are hurt (repressed) or ignored do not go away, but produce stronger negative feelings of bitterness.

A young soldier came to me for counseling. His wife had decided she didn't love her husband and was not certain she ever had. Was she in love with someone else? No—she had been true to him, but ten years before, he had confessed to her that when he had been overseas, in a time of loneliness and weakness, he had a sexual relationship with a girl who really didn't mean anything to him. A nasty argument had followed. Without applying forgiveness or resolving the issue, they had agreed "never to mention the incident again." There wasn't a day, however, when she didn't think of it, and until the situation was faced and resolved, there was no lessening the horrible turmoil that created stress in their marriage.

Attempting to ignore your emotions by saying, "Let's just not talk about it," or "Well, it was my fault as much as it was yours, so let's just forget it," doesn't resolve the problem. This is why the next step in making friends of your emotions is so important.

2. Get in Touch with Your Emotions

If you grew up in a family where emotional expression was taboo, you have to unlearn patterns of behavior, and this is difficult at best. For example, Russian males, as a rule of thumb, do not verbally express love or show physical affection. Yes, Russian men will greet each other with a kiss—an equivalent of a handshake; however, most Russian dads will never give their son a hug and say, "Son, I love you!"

But don't people know without being told? Possibly, but usually not.

That's why learning to express emotions is important—whether you write them, speak them, or rent an airplane and paint the sky with them.

Talking about emotions may not change things, but it changes your attitude toward what you cannot change. I remember returning home following the death and burial of my father. My in-laws, who were gracious, loving, and caring, never expressed a word of sympathy. Their silence, as though nothing had happened when someone important was taken from my life, was not only perplexing, it was annoying. Finally my wife asked her parents why they had not talked about Dad's home-going, and their response was that they didn't want to make me feel worse by talking about it. Nothing could be further from reality. Get in touch with your emotions and think about a way to bring expression to them.

3. Find Words to Describe and Express Your Emotions and Feelings

Though women find this easier to do than their male counterparts, talking about emotions and feelings is threatening to many people. Why? We feel vulnerable and fear rejection. It's like opening the door of a closet that has been nailed shut for years, something you can do only when you overcome your fear of being honest or believe that the rewards of open expression are greater than the possible consequences of "telling it like it is."

Psychologists (at least some of them) say there are six basic emotions: happiness, surprise, fear, sadness, disgust, and anger. And those who have studied them say there are over 600 words in English to describe them, and to express those emotions takes 42 facial muscles.

So where do you start? How do you constructively express your emotions? You can do it several ways. First, I suggest you relieve the pressure of those bottled-up emotions by talking about them to someone who is empathetic and nonjudgmental, someone who cares about you. Often men are more comfortable expressing emotions with other men in small groups. But developing intimacy between a husband and wife, both of whom are willing to express and describe their feelings, creates a stronger and often even more sexual bond between the two. There is great therapy in allowing someone to describe his or her feelings while the other listens.

At times I counsel someone and simply sit and listen for an hour. About all I contribute to the conversation is an occasional "Yes! I understand," "I see," or something else about as profound. But at the end of that hour the person will say, "You have helped me so much!" I didn't do anything but listen, but by allowing him the opportunity of getting something off his chest, I helped the person feel immensely better. He or she had expressed and externalized his or her emotions. I served as a sounding board, allowing the person to manifest the same emotions he would toward a person or situation that troubled him.

One of the Bible's profound psychological insights is that it clearly recognizes the importance of externalizing your emotions in proper ways. Jesus told us that if you have something against someone, or have a conflict with someone, you are to go to that person and share your conflict one to one (Matthew 18:15). By doing this you neither repress your emotions nor deny them. You externalize them! You deal with them in such a way that permanent relief is found from anger, hatred, or fear that can gnaw away at your viscera. Though we often try to avoid confrontation, at times it's vitally necessary in dealing with issues that must be faced.

Another thing you can do is to bring your burden and emotional fatigue to God in prayer. There's a big difference between sharing your concern with someone else and sharing it with God. You will feel better if you share your emotions with a friend, but all a friend can do is listen. When you share them with God, He can touch your heart and relieve the stress and strain you feel. But He doesn't stop there. He can also touch the hearts of those for whom you pray, allowing His divine power to melt and mold their hearts and lives to the configuration of His will.

The third stanza of the well-known hymn "What a Friend We Have in Jesus" is especially meaningful to this discussion:

> Are we weak and heavy laden,
>   Cumbered with a load of care?
> Precious Savior, still our Refuge!—
>   Take it to the Lord in pray'r.

> Do thy friends despise, forsake thee?
> Take it to the Lord in pray'r!
> In His arms He'll take and shield thee;
> Thou wilt find a solace there.

The words of Joseph Scriven's hymn reflect a painful experience he endured. The Canadian schoolteacher was engaged to be married, when an untimely accident took the life of the one he so loved. Unquestionably, Scriven wrote of the hiding place he had found in the friendship of a Savior who loved him and understood the pent-up emotions he couldn't express to others.

There is one who has faced the gamut of life's emotions from birth to death, and His name is Jesus. He knows how you feel when you find it so difficult to share, even with a husband or a wife. He knows and understands. When you pray, just open your heart and let the feelings flow out. Are you angry? Fearful? Discouraged? Confused? Do you think God doesn't know it? Then tell Him in no uncertain terms. No, you can't tell Him anything He does not already know, but asking Him to take over your burdens will bring peace to your troubled heart. James, the half brother of Jesus, was right when he wrote that we have not because we do not ask!

4. Trade In Your Unhealthy Emotions for Ones That Are Good for You

What I am asking you to consider is tough. Why? We hate turning loose of the familiar and habitual to develop new responses and allow new emotions to gradually root out the display of unhealthy ones. Clinging to the old patterns of behavior is less challenging than turning them loose. But consider the trapeze artist on the bar swinging through the air, gaining momentum with each pass—he's got to turn loose of the one bar and momentarily be suspended in air before he can grasp the one he's reaching for.

A rabbi who had lost his family in the Holocaust said that he forgave Hitler for the horrible loss he had sustained because he chose not to bring

Hitler to America with him. He knew that hatred did not destroy your enemy but caused your soul to die within you, something he chose not to pursue. He wisely chose to leave behind what needed to be discarded.

If you know you have no right to something but continue to focus on it, you feed emotions—hatred, lust, jealousy, envy, pride—that are counterproductive and wage war with your sense of rightness. How do you deal with this situation? Writing to the Corinthians, Paul told them to bring every thought captive to the obedience of Christ (2 Corinthians 10:5). If it helps, visualize bringing the negative emotion you struggle with—whatever it is that strives to take you captive—to a risen Savior and giving it to the One who reaches toward you in love.

5. Allow God to Invade Your Emotions

Evangelicals speak of inviting Jesus Christ to come into your heart as your Lord and Savior, something you possibly have already done. Often Revelation 3:20 is quoted, where Jesus says that He stands at the door of our heart and knocks, and that if you hear His voice and open the door, He will come in and have fellowship with you.

Vast numbers of people do that! They invite God to give them a new heart. Then they go one step further and recognize that God's Holy Spirit has come to indwell their lives, making their bodies the temples of the living God. But have you ever considered the importance of inviting Him to enter that chamber of your life known as your feelings and emotions?

In his book *Feel: The Power of Listening to Your Heart,* Matthew Elliott contends that society has created an emotional box—like a tomb with the stone rolled firmly against the door—and vast numbers of us are afraid of allowing God inside that box. Perhaps you are like that. Says Dr. Elliott,

> By barring God from the real emotional places of our lives, we rob him of his power. It's as if we tell him, "God, you won't do this in my life. I just know you won't. I can't have joy in this difficult tragedy. You won't be big enough to bring me to a place of contentment. I'm afraid you'll disappoint

me or fail me, and I can't take that chance." In this we keep God small.[4]

Instead of keeping your emotions confined to that box within, pray, "Lord, You have come into my life and my heart, but now I want to go one step further. I invite You to invade my emotions as well. I yield them to the control of Your Holy Spirit. Help me to use them in such a way that I glorify You and rejoice in how You created me." In doing this you make *friends* of your emotions, and doing that will make a tremendous difference in your life.

Yes, of course, that thought is scary! As a young man put it, "It is hard to trust an emotion as a friend when I am only meeting him for the very first time. He's like that cousin you had never met until the awkward family reunion."[5]

Remember, God is emotional, and when you allow Him to take control of your life, He'll also be in control of your emotions, working within, prompting, guiding you, helping you express yourself and glorify Him in the process. Never, ever forget that God is a good God, and what He does reflects that goodness and grace in your life.

QUESTIONS FOR THOUGHT AND DISCUSSION

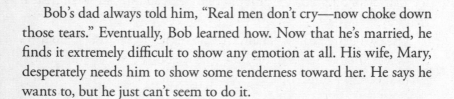

Bob's dad always told him, "Real men don't cry—now choke down those tears." Eventually, Bob learned how. Now that he's married, he finds it extremely difficult to show any emotion at all. His wife, Mary, desperately needs him to show some tenderness toward her. He says he wants to, but he just can't seem to do it.

    1. What is one thing Bob could do to start learning how to express his emotions rather than to repress them?

2. Take a look at your life. Name one sinful fear, one hatred, and one sinful anger. How can faith help you deal with that fear? How can love help you deal with that hatred? How can peace help you deal with that anger?

3. Which are you more likely to do—repress, deny, or externalize your emotions in a productive way? What are some steps you can take or are taking in a healthy direction?

This Will Hurt...

Stereotypes are not easily overcome. It is our cultural tendency for men to repress or deny emotions; it is the tendency for women to feel their way through situations. It will hurt if you continue to make excuses for yourself or others on the grounds that "men and women were created that way."

The two extremes we usually face are either to be tossed about on the waves of our emotions, or to be in dry dock. It will hurt to tip the balance in either direction.

This Will Help...

A person becomes very vulnerable when he expresses his emotions. In order to create a safe place for someone who is learning to express emotions, you must keep his confidence. Remember that the other person owns his emotions, and his sharing them with you does not give you permission to pass them out to whomever you choose.

Learning to make *I feel* statements instead of *you* statements will help in two ways. First, it will help keep communication between two people clear. Rather than accusing, "When you do that, you make me feel _____" say, "I feel _____ when that happens." *I feel* statements also help you identify what it is you are feeling instead of focusing on what the other person is doing.

Chapter 5

Memories That Burn

What happens when you cannot forget? Ask Jill Price, a 42-year-old woman, and she can tell you precisely! Why? Known as "The Woman Who Can't Forget," she has almost total recall of every day of her life, starting in childhood.

Price's phenomenal ability to recall was first described in 2006, when James L. McGaugh, a professor of neurobiology at the University of California, Irvine, went public with a five-year study he had conducted with her, bombarding her with a wide variety of psychological, neurological, and physiological tests to learn why she had such amazing recall. For example, when she was asked what she did on October 19, 1979, she would recall, "I came home from school and had soup because it was unusually cold that day." Jerry Adler, writing for *Newsweek* magazine, reports that October 19, 1979, was, in fact, cloudy with a high of 67 in Los Angeles, well below normal. Says Dr. McGaugh, "She doesn't make it up or fake it."[1]

Most of us, however, seldom remember what we had for lunch last week. However, there are certain memories—some good, but many that we would like to forget—that are burned into the folds of our brain. Why Jill Price's brain, along with those of several other individuals who have almost total recall, works that way with nearly every event is something neuroscientists haven't quite figured out.

The human brain is an amazing phenomenon. It consists of about 100 billion nerve units known as *neurons,* which are surrounded by a mass, 90 percent by bulk, of *glial cells—glia* being the Greek word for *glue.* The average adult human brain weighs about three pounds. In the part called the *cerebrum,* where we do our thinking, lies the temporal lobe, which concerns itself with our emotions and memory. Even with all the knowledge that science has acquired about the human brain, there is still much that is unknown.

One thing we do know is that the human brain processes more than 10,000 thoughts every day. Though scientists say it is far superior to any computer ever invented, it is actually unfair to even suggest a comparison to a computer. No computer, regardless of its sophistication, can rival the human brain, with its vast scope of emotions and comprehension.

There is, however, a function of computers which I sometimes wish the human brain had, something I mentioned previously: the ability to input a command that would erase those things we would like to forget. Shock therapy, used predominately in the 1950s and early 1960s, was an attempt to electrically remove certain events or memories that cause grief and pain.

But God has a better way—the healing of the emotions.

Memories That Scar Our Lives Are Commonplace

From a 70-year-old woman came the following letter:

> I was so interested in what you said about memories and how they can ruin the joy we should have in our Christian walk. I am 70 years old and have lived a full and eventful life and have, as you might probably know, memories that both bless and burn, a few that hurt deeply, and you helped

me to feel I might be able to get rid of the ones that have burned so deeply.

Memories that burn, as this woman described them, are the ones that come back to haunt you and rob you of your peace of mind and create those inner struggles that dog some people for an entire lifetime. I know that was true of a pastor friend of mine whose wife faced the prospect of either having surgery or spending the rest of her life as an invalid in a wheelchair. The two of them talked and prayed, sought counsel, and weighed the odds in their minds, trying to visualize how they would cope with life if she would never be able to walk again.

Confident that God would see her through, they opted for surgery, which failed. When she died as the result of complications on the operating table, the pastor took it as a personal failure. He was absolutely convinced he was responsible for her death by allowing her to face the surgery. Her death became a memory that not only burned, but scarred his life so deeply that he was unable to carry on his work. In defeat and shock he resigned from his church, left the ministry, and began to drift from one job to another.

The parents of a four-year-old boy also found it very difficult to find healing for their self-imposed responsibility for his death. While the family was vacationing in northern California, the dad saw a highway sign pointing to a campground. Turning to his wife he said, "What do you think?"

> What happened deeply burned their memories and left wounds that could be healed only by the grace of God.

"I'm so tired," she said, "let's stop."

He paused for a moment and then replied, "I'd sure like to get in a few more miles before we quit for the night." He shifted gears and rolled on down the highway.

In the back of the camper, their tired little boy crawled up into the sleeping area over the cab and went to sleep. Only a short distance down the road there was a sudden snap, and the rear axle of their pickup broke in a freakish accident that caused the vehicle to lurch one way and then the other, finally turning over. The mom and dad crawled out of the tangled wreckage and frantically tried to free their little boy, who had been trapped. Moments after he was freed, the little fellow breathed his last in the arms of his daddy.

His funeral was one of the saddest I have ever conducted. The sight of a little boy with a shock of blond curls over his forehead resting in a four-foot casket, his "wooly" and his teddy bear cradled in one arm, absolutely tore out my heart.

What made the loss all the more difficult was that the father felt totally responsible for what had happened. "It was all my fault," he reasoned. "If I had listened to my wife, we would have stopped earlier and our little boy would still be alive." Talk about painful inner struggles!

Sure, you can reason, "Neither the pastor nor the dad was actually responsible." Nonetheless, what happened deeply burned their memories and left wounds that could be healed only by the grace of God.

Perhaps your inner struggle is totally different, the result of having been hurt by another, possibly someone you deeply loved, someone whom you thought would never hurt you. Perhaps it was your father when you were a child, or later in life your wife or husband. Perhaps it was an angry argument with your son or daughter, broken faith with your mate, or something you did that nobody knows about except you. Whatever it is, it is a wound that deeply hurt you.

"A few years back," wrote a husband, "my wife was having an affair with another man and I caught her. I forgave her," he said, "but every time she is more than an hour late coming home, I feel she is out doing the same thing. I am trying to trust her again. Please pray for me and send me some literature on this to help me with the problem. I am trying to forget and I have forgiven her. It was about eight years ago…"

I have no doubt that every person who reads this page can sift back through the years and ponder some "memory that burns" that has created traumatic inner struggles. As the immediate trauma subsided, you probably prayed for God's forgiveness for what you did, or think you did, to contribute to the problem. Most of the time, you probably believe that God has forgiven you, but there may be times when you are not really sure.

Even if you know that God has forgiven you, it is certainly possible you haven't forgiven yourself. It is quite often far more difficult to forgive ourselves than to seek and find the forgiveness of God.

No matter what happened to burn your memory, you must follow certain steps to realize and experience healing of your emotions.

Guideline 1: You Need to Understand the Nature of Forgiveness

When it comes to living harmoniously, no other quality, with the possible exception of love, is more needed than forgiveness. It is in our daily routines that the irritations of our human faults and imperfections take their toll. Abrasiveness causes an oyster to produce a pearl, but in people, too much abrasion produces wounds.

In marriage, forgiveness is a storm wall that keeps the winds from blowing down the house. The more you love someone, the more you strive to live so it isn't necessary to ask forgiveness. But no man or woman is so perfect that at times he doesn't find himself in the position of needing what alone can bring healing to a relationship—forgiveness.

This healing balm is really a reminder of our human frailties. If a person could so live that he would neither offend nor be an offense to someone, he would never find himself in the position of having to say, "I'm sorry, forgive me." But the individual who realizes his own weakness should gladly extend the priceless balm of forgiveness because he can understand that his own faults and failures will eventually demand that he ask for the same thing.

The work of gratitude. When you forgive another, you acknowledge a deeper debt of gratitude—that of gratitude to God Himself. Jesus well illustrated this when He told a story of a certain slave who owed a rather large debt to his master. The master, out of the goodness of his heart, forgave the man; however, when a fellow citizen owed a very small amount to the slave who had been forgiven and could not pay, the slave demanded that the fellow be thrown in prison until he could repay the debt (see Matthew 18:21-35).

We're like that. We are often quick to expect the other to forgive us, but we are slow to extend forgiveness to someone we think owes us. Jesus said plainly that if we do not forgive each other, neither will our Father in heaven forgive us (Matthew 6:15).

Paul, too, stressed our greater debt to God when he wrote to both the Ephesians and the Colossians saying that we must forgive each other, even as God for Christ's sake has forgiven us.

How far should you go when it comes to forgiving someone? Forgiveness of any kind is so contrary to the way most of us think today. How often do we think, *Give the so-and-so a taste of his own medicine! Divorce the lout! File charges and put him in the slammer! Isn't an "eye for an eye and a tooth for a tooth" in the Bible?*

Peter asked Jesus, "How often should I forgive my brother? Seven times?" That was really quite generous of Peter, for the rabbis taught that three times was enough, and then if someone did the same thing again, he was to be treated as an enemy for life. But Jesus was quite plain: "Seventy times seven!" Our tendency is to think, *Aha! A coupon book with 490 stubs, and then when they are gone, pow!* That is not the point Jesus was making. Neither 7 nor 490! Jesus is telling us very plainly that there must be no end to this matter of forgiveness (see Matthew 18:21-22)!

Letting go. There is a meaningful picture surrounding the word that the writers of Scripture used regarding the necessity of forgiveness. The Greek word *aphiami,* usually translated "to forgive," also means "to throw," or "to let go." In time it came to mean "to send" or "to give up."

The word was used in legal writing when the governor forgave his subjects of back taxes that were owed to the state. It was used of criminals who had been forgiven by the government, and then it was used frequently in Scripture to stress the importance of learning to forgive each other. When it comes to the need for forgiveness, the real point is not how badly you have been hurt, but rather that you are willing to give up your claim to compensation for what someone has done to you.

Scripture gives many poignant illustrations of what forgiveness is. Psalm 103:12 says that when God forgives us, our sins are as far removed from us as the east is from the west. The image intended is that the east and the west never meet.

In Micah 7, the writer uses the picture of the deepest sea into which God casts our sins. The deepest part of the ocean is found in the Mariana

Trench off Saipan in the Pacific, where the ocean is some 35,000 feet deep—or deeper than the height of Mount Everest, the highest mountain in the world. Though that is a great distance, you still would not find all of your sins and failures piled there. You could take a bathyscaphe, a little submarine with which scientists explore the depths of the ocean, and you could get to the deepest point, but you would still not find them.

Guideline 2: Be Sure You Have Sought God's Forgiveness for Your Own Life

There are times when failures drive us to our knees, when our own behavior makes us realize that our hearts are deceptive and sinful. Scores of people have written to me and told how marital failures or personal tragedies caused them to realize that there was a spiritual emptiness in them, and that through this they turned to God and became a Christian. This letter is typical:

> I'd like your help in learning how to let Christ into my life, to accept Him as my personal Savior. I thought I had several months ago following a severe family upheaval involving sin on my part. I had asked forgiveness of the Lord and felt I'd received it, but my wife says she cannot forgive. My wife and I love each other—she feels it would be against her principles to stay with me, but I don't want her to go. We're both miserable. Did the Lord really forgive me and is this punishment for my sins? Please help me.

Personal failures always cause us to doubt our relationship with God. If you have never established a relationship with Jesus Christ as your personal Savior, you will have unrest in your heart, and your emotions are bound to be troubled. If this is a picture of your life, then pray a simple, meaningful, prayer right now:

"Heavenly Father, something is wrong with my life and I know it is the sin of my heart. I want You to forgive me and I want You to come into my life and let Jesus be my Savior right now." (See John 1:12; Acts 16:31; Romans 10:9,13; and Titus 3:5.)

If there is something specific, something you are troubled by that you know was sin in the sight of God, then remember 1 John 1:9: "If we confess our sins, he is faithful and just and will forgive us our sins and purify us from all unrighteousness." Mention that sin, and in prayer confess it before God; then realize that because He promised to forgive you, you can be assured He has kept His word and no longer holds that against you.

Briefly, there are four liberating truths about God's forgiveness you need to know:

God's forgiveness is unconditional. You don't need to embark upon a self-improvement plan before you are good enough to come to God and ask His help. It isn't necessary for you to first clean up your act so you might be worthy of an audience with the Great King. The only obstacle is your own reluctance to come to Him. Isaiah 1:18 is still valid:

> "Come now, let us reason together," says the LORD. "Though your sins are like scarlet, they shall be as white as snow; though they are red as crimson, they shall be like wool."

Jesus gave a carte blanche invitation: "Whoever comes to me I will never drive away" (John 6:37).

God's forgiveness is unlimited in scope. Some believe that God's forgiveness may cover the first offense, but after a couple or three repeats, they begin to question whether the invitation is still good.

Others believe that certain deeds such as abortion, adultery, fornication, homosexuality, and so on, are unforgivable. Both concepts are untrue.

Paul catalogues numerous deeds which would fall into the second category. Then he says, "And that is what some of you were. But you were washed, you were sanctified, you were justified in the name of the Lord Jesus Christ and by the Spirit of our God" (1 Corinthians 6:11). Therefore, it must be recognized that there is no limitation on the kinds of sins God will forgive when we come to Him.

God's forgiveness is absolute. Unlike our human memories, God wipes the slate clean as though it had never happened. Isaiah 43:25 put it like this, "I, even I, am he who blots out your transgressions, for my own sake, and remembers your sins no more."

"You mean that I will never have to give an account for the abortion that I had?" a woman who had just prayed to receive Jesus Christ as her Savior blurted. Three broken marriages followed by an unwanted pregnancy had left her in a terrible state of despair. Thinking that an abortion was the only way out, she battled her conscience, weighing the thought of ending the struggling life within her body against her ability to survive as a single mother of two older children plus a newborn. As the nurse wheeled the gurney down the hospital corridor, with glistening tears streaming down her cheeks she cried out, "Oh, God, have I really come to this?" And right then she vowed that some way, somehow she would make the matter right with God.

I explained that when God forgives, He wipes out our wrongs and transgressions as though we had never sinned. Then she rephrased her question—"You mean I'll never have to face God because of what I did?"

"Never again!" I explained, and I showed her that Peter says Christ bore our sins in His body on the tree (see 1 Peter 2:24). The price has already been paid, which means that because God allowed Christ to be treated as we should have been treated, He will treat us for all eternity as Christ should have been treated. That's good news!

God's forgiveness is redemptive. "If I asked God to forgive me before I took an overdose of drugs," asked a deeply disturbed woman who had given up on living, "would He forgive me so I wouldn't go to hell?" On occasion I have had teenagers sit in my office and, with full understanding of what they were about to do, say, "I know God will forgive me, so I'm going to go right ahead and do it."

Often overlooked is one tremendous fact: When Jesus reaches out to someone in need and says, "I forgive you!" He also adds, "Now, go and sin no more." There is power in those words, a strength which helps an individual rise above the force or pull which would drag him down again. Forgiveness brings a motive for saying, "No! I have to break this off. I just cannot continue to do this."

Guideline 3: Extend Forgiveness to the One Who Has Hurt You

Once you have squared things away with God, take a look at your relationship with other people. The next step in the process is to forgive anyone who has hurt you. There is something you need to know, something extremely important: Forgiveness does not mean, "What you did to me is okay!" What was done to you was wrong—not okay for a moment. Rather, forgiveness means, "I give up my right to hurt you because you hurt me." It means you take the wrong and put it in the hand of God, saying, "God, You handle this. I refuse to become bitter and angry over this!"

In a small out-of-the-way cemetery in upper New York is a tombstone bearing the single word: "FORGIVEN!" Nothing more or less, just "forgiven"! That single word on an otherwise unmarked grave is like a big question mark. What was forgiven? And by whom? Did some wrongdoing cause someone to seek out the grave of a person whose identity was eventually lost to posterity and add that word, "forgiven"?

Maybe it was a wife who, for many years, harbored resentment or perhaps even hatred in her heart toward a husband who had been unfaithful, a husband who had left her and the children for someone whose beauty was not faded with the toil of raising offspring.

Perhaps it was a father who had angry words with his son. Maybe the son had packed his few belongings in a rickety suitcase and walked down the dusty road leading to the big city, only to be struck down, a prodigal who would never return. Maybe the father sought out the grave so he could let the world know that the son had been forgiven.

Or perhaps it was nothing so melodramatic at all. Perhaps someone simply wanted the world to know he had tasted richly of God's great grace, and that he had been forgiven!

Forgiven! The very word smacks of heaven itself, and perhaps that is why it so very difficult to forgive—to say nothing of forgetting. Have you ever faced a situation when you had been so hurt that you absolutely could not bring yourself to forgive? If so, you have had plenty of company down through the years.

When you think you can't forgive. How do you overcome bitterness and hatred when you have been wronged and are absolutely convinced you cannot forgive? If you find yourself in the position of not being able to forgive another person, yet at the same time you know that

God expects you to forgive as He forgives you, then read the next few paragraphs carefully.

The first step is to come to grips with the simple fact that you can't forgive a person in your own strength. You must bring the problem to the Lord. Most of the time we avoid letting God know that we would really like to see the offender "get it in the neck." We just carry on our polite conversations with Him, rather than really coming to the place where we admit, "God, I just can't forgive that one."

The second step is to begin to pray for the person who has hurt you, the one you can't forgive. Does that put you on a pinnacle of virtue as you look down on the other? Jesus prayed, "Father, forgive them…" As you pray for someone, you gradually begin to feel pity for the one who has harmed you. You begin to see him as a human being who is weak and frail—as totally human. Your feelings of hatred will begin to turn to pity, and finally the feelings of pity are replaced by a tenderness that allows you to forgive him.

This doesn't mean that you would necessarily want to spend the rest of your life on a deserted island with the individual who has hurt you. It does mean that your stomach no longer knots when you see that person or think about him. Your lip no longer curls when his name is mentioned.

Confrontation. Ultimately, there needs to be confrontation with any person you have hurt, one in which you say, "I'm sorry; will you forgive me?" Ideally, the person who hurt you will come to the same place with himself. This is not a step we like. If forgiveness could be extended or received without any personal contact it would be much easier. But eventually we all need to face uncomfortable issues in our lives if we want to grow. Facing the issue demands facing the individual with whom we have conflicts.

> Sending a gift or letting another person be your advocate…doesn't complete the transaction.

When you think, *I can't forgive someone,* try to remember that forgiveness is first a matter of the will, then a matter of the emotions. You can say, "Yes, I will forgive _____; I make the decision in my head," and then you will find that your heart follows.

Jesus was very clear when He said that if another person sins against you, you are to go to him alone and tell him his fault. Sending a gift or letting another person be your advocate may be a good gesture on your part, but it doesn't complete the transaction until you say, "Please forgive me," or "I have forgiven you, and I want you to do the same for me."

Guideline 4: You Must Forgive Yourself

Forgiveness is like a three-legged stool. If any one of the three "legs" is missing, forgiveness is incomplete. The three crucial parts are 1) your relationship to God, 2) your relationship to the offended person or persons, and 3) your relationship to yourself. It is this last area, perhaps, that causes the greatest inner struggles. Undoubtedly, many people find it easier to pour out their hearts to God, to seek and find His forgiveness, than to forgive themselves. Consider the burden of these people:

> I am 20 years old and have been divorced for three years and have done some bad sins. Jesus says, "If we confess our sins, He'll be faithful to forgive us," but at times I just can't forgive myself and want to die.

Another writes:

> I know that what the Bible says is so true; but 15 years ago I disobeyed God's commandment and committed adultery. My husband has forgiven me, but I just can't seem to find peace of mind. I can't seem to think of anything else. What can I do?

Yet another says,

> I accepted the Lord Jesus Christ as my personal Savior some 20 years ago. It seems I have been running from myself ever since. I am the most frustrated, confused, defeated individual you will ever hear about. I have a wonderful family, wife, three boys, and one daughter—all saved, everything. Yet, I am so miserable. You said something on your program this morning

that may be my problem. In essence what you said was, "God
has forgiven you, but you can't forgive yourself..."

Hundreds of people are like this—relatively sure that God has forgiven them, but unable to let themselves off the hook. If you are like that,
begin by asking yourself a somewhat philosophical question: *What right
do I have to refuse to forgive myself when God has forgiven me?* We'd all
agree, theoretically, that there is no right. Your failing to forgive yourself
destroys your peace of mind, and further, it diminishes your effectiveness
because you bear an incredible burden of guilt. This is not a guilt that
God intended for you to carry.

Guideline 5: Give the Bitterness of That Memory to Jesus

Why should you carry the burden of a memory that burns and scars,
when Jesus already died for the very burden you are trying to carry? It
simply is not your responsibility.

When I talk to people about whether or not they have a right to hold
a grudge against themselves, I often ask them, "If you understand that
God has forgiven you, what right do you think you have not to forgive
yourself? Are you greater than He?" They usually smile and say, "I see
how ridiculous it is." It is because you care that you punish yourself. But
your failing to forgive yourself robs you of peace of mind. It destroys your
ability to function properly, and certainly saps you of spiritual vitality. It
is a burden that God doesn't want you to bear, and in a very real sense it
renders what Christ did of no effect because you bear the guilt of your
failure, one that He bore long ago.

You need to take positive action to rid yourself of that guilt once and
for all, to get things into perspective. First, in your mind's eye, picture
Jesus as He hung on the cross with all the suffering and loneliness He
endured. It is not a pleasant picture. There is an inscription posted above
Him—one that didn't make the Jews very happy. It read, "This is Jesus,
the King of Jews," and it was written in Hebrew, Greek, and Aramaic
(see Matthew 27:37). The very act itself was part of the crucifixion ritual

instituted by the Romans. Trying to make the offending person a public example, the Romans had a custom of writing the crime for which the person was executed on parchment or papyrus and placing it on the cross so all who passed by would know why the person was being executed.

Now, think about the memory that burns, the sin or deed that troubles you, as if it were written on a piece of parchment and affixed to the cross as the crime for which Jesus died. Picture the blood that flowed from His wounds covering that writing until it is obliterated forever.

Paul painted the picture of our sins being obliterated like that when he wrote to the Colossians,

> When you were dead in your sins and in the uncircumcision of your sinful nature, God made you alive with Christ. He forgave us all our sins, having canceled the written code, with its regulations, that was against us and that stood opposed to us; he took it away, nailing it to the cross (Colossians 2:13-14).

This is not mental hocus-pocus or conjuring up memories of bitterness that do not exist but you wish would happen, like something New Age adherents call *visualization*. Rather, viewing yourself and your sin from God's perspective is part of faith. No wonder the author of Hebrews wrote, "Faith is being sure of what we hope for and certain of what we do not see" (Hebrews 11:1).

Another way you can help rid your memory of bitterness that burns your soul is to sit down and write out the memory in detail. Write out the sordid details, but do it in private. Now take the memorandum and crumple it up in a ball; and in your mind's eye, picture Jesus standing in front of you and give it to Him. See His nail-scarred hands taking the memorandum from you so you will never face it again. As you do this, literally give the memory to Him. Remember, from God's vantage point, it is already gone. Forgiven! He gave us a promise: "I, even I, am the one who wipes out your transgression for My own sake. And I will not remember your sins" (Isaiah 43:25 NASB).

It may help to touch a match to the paper you have written, and as the flames lick it up, remind yourself that you, as a conscious act of the will, gave that memory to Jesus. Then, leave it in His hands.

Guideline 6: Refuse to Let Your Mind Dwell on the Memory That Burns

When 14-year-old Elizabeth Smart was kidnapped from her Salt Lake home by a local drifter named Brian David Mitchell, it made news around the world. For nine long months this charming girl was kept in chains, sexually assaulted, and otherwise abused. But she never gave up hope. Six years afterward, Elizabeth described her ordeal to Cathy Free and Alex Tresniowski of *People* magazine. They say,

> After her rescue, the key to her readjustment was letting go of the hate she felt toward her abductors. Said Elizabeth, "Nine months of my life had been taken from me, and I wasn't going to give them any more of my time."

No matter how hard it is, you are the loser when you can't let go of some memories. Letting go is the key to restoring emotional normalcy.

Some folks live with constant bitterness and heartache because they cling to the shattered fragments of a life that went to pieces. At every opportunity, they tell their story—and if an opportunity doesn't come up, they make one! Eventually, their friends no longer want to hear it, and avoid them. Loneliness compounds the hurt. If God has forgiven you, and if you have forgiven yourself, and if you have forgiven those who may have hurt you, refuse to let your mind dwell on the matter. Satan often defeats us by bringing to our minds things that have been forgiven and must be forgotten.

Guideline 7: Replace the Memory That Burns with the Word of God

There is healing in the Word of God itself. The Holy Spirit uses the Word to bring restoration and healing to burned-out emotions. Dave Wilkerson, author of the book *The Cross and the Switchblade,* said that the most effective therapy for a person who has burned out his mind with drugs is to begin to program his mind with God's Word, the Bible. This brings psychological and spiritual healing. He is not alone in that claim, either. And it has been my experience that the same applies not only to individuals whose minds have been dulled by drugs but also to individuals who have burned out emotionally.

Guideline 8: Cooperate with the Holy Spirit in Your Healing

Be very certain of this fact: When you search the catalog of virtues or characteristics of the Spirit-filled life (Galatians 5:22-23), you will not find bitterness listed among them. You will, however, find it listed among the descriptions of the flesh immediately preceding. Simply put, bitterness is not from the Lord, and your cooperation with the Holy Spirit to allow God to touch your life is very important.

It is the nature of Satan to ensnare, deceive, and destroy, while it is the nature of God to liberate and bring restoration and healing. It is a defective theology that believes God is interested in extending forgiveness alone to a person, leaving his emotional life still stunted and twisted by memories that burn. Emotional healing is an intrinsic part of the redemptive plan of God. He told His children right out, "I am the LORD who heals you" (Exodus 15:26). David spoke of the Lord as the one "who forgives all your sins and heals all your diseases" (Psalm 103:3). This has to include the healing of the memory and emotions as well as the physical body.

If you mean business about finding God's healing power for your emotions and memories that burn, and you still have not found relief, I suggest that you take the next step, which is outlined in James 5:14. Call upon the elders of your local congregation and ask them to anoint you with oil and to pray for emotional healing. It isn't necessary to share the details of what troubles you, but it is helpful to have someone else pray for you in order to have complete healing.

If you are not in a church, if there is none near you, have several other Christians join you and ask them to pray according to the outline of James 5. You might say, "Well, I can pray for myself." Yes, you can. But there is much to be said for the power of corporate prayer. There are times when you don't have the faith to believe God for yourself. You are the one who has taken it on the chin emotionally, and you might feel you can't get it all together on your own. Praying with another person will compound your faith.

How is that? I'm not sure that I can explain the *how* of it, but the *why* of it was laid down by Jesus:

> I tell you that if two of you on earth agree about anything you ask for, it will be done for you by my Father in heaven. For where two or three come together in my name, there am I with them (Matthew 18:19-20).

For far too long, many churches have looked the other way regarding the power of God in healing the body, the emotions, and the soul. Perhaps it is because of the quacks and professional "healers" who have prostituted the power of God for their own selfish purposes. Even so, we must assume the privilege, as well as the responsibility, of attending to the needs of the whole man. We must redeem our spiritual birthright and heritage that we have in Jesus Christ.

Guideline 9: Begin Thanking God for Bringing Restoration and Healing to Your Life

When fire swept through Laguna Canyon near our office, one of the properties affected was the Hortense Miller Garden, a botanical garden containing more than 2000 varieties of plants and flowers. The place was a veritable paradise of beautiful blooms and greenery. The fire, of course, blackened the hillside and left its ugly scars. Disaster? Yes! That's what people called it, and rightly so. Yet, as I am writing this, months later, the hills are alive with the beauty of wildflowers that have not been seen in the area for a generation or more.

You see, years ago, before the area was converted into a garden, wildflowers covered the hillside. But these gave way to domestic plants and shrubs, which soon took over the sunlight and snagged nourishment from the soil. The seeds of the wildflowers, however, lay in the ground—some 30 to 40 years, some even 75 or 100 years. They were dormant but not dead. Then came the fire, a disaster from the human standpoint. It burned most things to the ground, allowing the sunlight and the rain to penetrate to the dormant wild seeds. They then sprang up in resurrection beauty.

"I wasn't too happy about it," Mrs. Miller, founder of the garden, said about the fire, "but...I think this is exciting." Today, it's different from the formal, more stately garden that existed before the fire, but the beauty is still there—rearranged by God's own hand. What appeared to us to be a disaster gave the area a different sort of beauty, one that could be produced only by the hand of God Himself.

There is a difference between a Christian and the person who considers life a disorganized and disconnected move of fate. The Christian knows—or should know—that God's purpose and design is behind every event, even though he cannot see the pattern at the time. The Christian looks for the wildflowers after the fire, and he can accept the fact that God is working all things after the pattern of His will (see Ephesians 1:11; Romans 8:28).

Let Him work in your life. Begin to thank Him for the restoration and healing that can follow the fire. Then begin to look for the flowers that can transform the blackened landscape of life into a wild and colorful garden.

The wildflowers are sure to come.

QUESTIONS FOR THOUGHT AND DISCUSSION

———— ꙮ ————

Alicia was happily married and the mother of two darling girls. After ten years of marriage, her husband, Jim, began to grow distant. He spent more and more time away from home, and when he was home he usually escaped into the TV. Alicia's world collapsed when Jim announced he had never really loved her, was tired of living a lie, and wanted a divorce so he could marry another woman, who worked in his office. Alicia now lies awake nights, replaying the fact that she was pregnant when she and

Jim were married. Even though Jim hadn't wanted to get married at first, they did, and he had seemed happy until he dropped his bomb.

1. What are some of the ways Alicia might blame herself? What are two things she can do in order to deal with the pain and betrayal so the result is not bitterness?

2. Think of one thing that used to be a memory that burned in your mind, but no longer is so. What was the process you went through in order to get rid of the bitterness or guilt?

3. What is one memory that is still burning into your mind, either something you did or something that was done to you? What are three things you can do—either what has worked for you in the past or something you learned from this chapter—to start the healing process?

This Will Hurt...

Replaying the emotional tapes over and over in your mind will only compound guilt, frustration, anger, and any other negative emotion. It will keep you focused on assigning blame. It will hurt to hold your bitterness to you, because bitterness eats at your soul like acid and spills out onto other people.

This Will Help...

Many people find that some pain is too big to face alone. You might want to get counseling, or talk to a good friend. It will help to remember that healing is a process and that it will take time.

You can try this exercise: Write out exactly how you feel—put all of your anger and bitterness down on paper. Then light a match and touch it to the paper. As you watch the flames erase the words, remind yourself that you can let go of the feelings they expressed. Ask God to help you leave the ashes with Him.

CHAPTER 6

Anger—Friend or Foe?

Back in the days when businessmen took trains rather than flying to appointments, a certain Illinois businessman, who was extremely tired and a very sound sleeper, was concerned he would oversleep and fail to get off at his destination. He gave a porter a large tip, asking if he would be sure to put him off the train the next morning at 5 a.m. at Deer Park. He explained he had a very important engagement and was afraid he would not wake up.

"Yes, sir!" replied the porter, "I can take care of it for you!"

But at 9 a.m. the next morning, the businessman awakened to discover he was still on the train and was at least 200 miles beyond Deer Park. It was a very angry man who found the porter and gave him a verbal tongue-lashing, throwing in a few words he hadn't used since his Navy days, before he stomped off the train.

"That absolutely has to be the maddest man I have ever seen," replied the conductor, who happened to be standing nearby.

"Boy, if you think he was mad," replied the porter, "you should have seen the man I put off the train this morning at 5 a.m.!"

We smile at the incident, but the number of people today who allow anger to get the best of them is no laughing matter. Are we an angry generation? Has stress torqued the rubber bands of our inner ability to stretch so that issues worth only a pinch of adrenaline turn into major displays of emotion?

Anger Is on the Increase

Displays of anger, both public and private, are on the increase. Dr. James Comer, Professor of Child Psychiatry at Yale University, who has served in Yale University's School of Medicine since 1968, characterized us as in "an 'angry age'—much more so than at any time in history."[1]

If you question whether displays of anger are on the increase, notice what happens when somebody cuts in front of another car at the gas pump, or what happens when somebody pushes somebody in a crowded elevator, or steps in front of somebody in a checkout line in a grocery store. Displays of road rage have become so serious that motor vehicle consultants advise caution in tapping the horn if the car in front of you doesn't move when the light changes, or flicking your lights when an oncoming motorist has his lights on bright. Why? Tempers flare, and fast!

> Is temper both an ally... as well as a potentially devastating force?

Most of us have grown up feeling that anger is a potentially dangerous emotion, and that any display of anger is always wrong—but is it really? Is it bad to get mad? Or is temper both an ally—something powerful that if used properly is very positive—as well as a potentially devastating force that can destroy and damage relationships? Is temper a two-edged sword?

Is It Bad to Get Mad?

The answer to the question "Is it bad to get mad?" is this: It all depends on how you handle it, how you direct it. Frankly, individuals who never get angry about anything don't amount to much and care very little about life. Steel without temper is worthless, and individuals without a measure of temper fail to make much of an impact in terms of character and uprightness.

Surprising as it is to some folks, the Bible has a great deal to say about anger, or strong wrath. In the Old Testament alone there are 455 references to anger; of those, 375 are references to God Himself.[2] Many of those references are in relationship to His own people, Israel, who refused to follow His direction. The result was that God was displeased—yes, no less than angry with them, because of it.

"Who can stand before you when you are angry?" asked the psalmist in Psalm 76:7. Nahum, the prophet who chronicled the fall of ancient Nineveh, asked, "Who can withstand his indignation? Who can endure his fierce anger?" adding, "His wrath is poured out like fire; the rocks are shattered before him" (Nahum 1:6). The New Testament writer of the book of Hebrews reflects on the intensity of an angry God, saying, "It is a dreadful thing to fall into the hands of the living God" (Hebrews 10:31). Noteworthy is the fact that the Bible says more about God's anger and wrath than about His love and mercy!

Jesus' anger. Was Jesus ever angry? Indeed, He was. On several occasions He was angry with His disciples, who refused to believe Him. He became angry with the Pharisees because of the hardness of their hearts and their hypocrisy. Whitened sepulchers "full of dead men's bones" was Jesus' description of them. His anger was obvious when He overturned the tables of the money changers and the benches of those selling doves in the temple. Picking up a whip He drove them out. "'My house will be called a house of prayer,'" He said, "but you are making it a 'den of robbers'" (Matthew 21:13).

Have you ever asked yourself a question that I have often pondered—especially when I'm on a flight trying to use my computer or study and the kid sitting in the seat behind me keeps kicking my seat with his feet, and his mother ignores the situation—what would make Jesus angry if He were here today? Would it be having to wait a bit longer at the airport check-in kiosk when someone pushes in front of Him? Would He get angry when someone picked up the remote control and changed the program He was watching on TV? Would global warming or higher prices at the gas pump irk Him? I can tell you something for sure: Most of what gnaws at our viscera wouldn't bother Him a bit.

On the other hand, I suspect He would be quite angry over some situations that hardly cause a ripple of indignation among us today, such as the number of broken homes that tear families apart, the number of abortions taking place, the lack of integrity in public and private life, the emasculation of men that results in vast numbers of kids being raised without a dad, injustices that are forced upon people, and greed and waste (to mention but a few things)—wrongdoing that is ignored by most of us.

It's your choice. The Bible makes it clear that anger, like a scalpel in the hands of a skilled surgeon, is amoral; it can either be harmful and wrong, or used properly it can be a powerful motivation for character and integrity.

The writers of Scripture refer to strong anger as "wrath," and almost always it is referred to in a negative context. Paul wrote, "God did not appoint us to suffer wrath but to receive salvation through our Lord Jesus Christ" (1 Thessalonians 5:9). Wrath—strong anger—usually works against us, provoking us to do things we later regret. James, the half brother of Jesus, wrote, "Man's anger does not bring about the righteous life that God desires" (James 1:20).

The Bible clearly differentiates between *being angry* and *remaining angry*. "In your anger do not sin" was Paul's guideline to the Ephesians (see Ephesians 4:26). Therefore, it is how you handle anger—not whether you have it—that determines whether it is right or wrong.

Where Does Anger Come From?

Why is it that we are an angry, uptight generation? To make it personal, why do you allow your temper to flare on occasion? Why should we be angry, when we have so much that previous generations didn't have? For a few minutes, think with me about some of the factors that produce emotional outbursts, which often explode at the slightest spark of provocation.

1. Stress produces anger. We live busier lives today than at any time in recent history, and tension is the result. Like the string of a violin that is tightened and tightened until it snaps, we load our schedules tighter and tighter until we explode in a burst of anger and then ask ourselves, "Why did I let myself get so mad?" It's simple—you compressed too much into a short span of time, and then you feel guilty because you are convinced that "spiritual folks" just don't get angry. But you did, and then you were upset with yourself because of it.

You may be trying to do what Jesus Himself could not do—live without proper rest and relaxation. He told His disciples to "come apart and rest awhile" after their labors. But you don't allow yourself time to do that. However, if you don't learn to "come apart and rest awhile," you'll just come apart, and you won't like it when it happens. (In chapter 9 we will take an in-depth look at stress and how it affects our lives.)

Vast numbers of people today feel that the stress of life is compounded by their inability to do anything about it—which leads to my next point.

2. Frustration produces outbursts of anger. I know. It happened to me recently, and while I like to think of myself as a "pretty much in control" sort of person, my response—okay, my anger—surprised me. I was returning from an overseas period of ministry and stopped in Korea for a couple of days of relaxation and shopping with my wife.

Not wanting to run out of money, I had carefully allocated what I needed for the brief stay, even down to the cost of the taxi, the tip for the porters who carried the suitcases, and enough to buy lunch before our departure. Making sure I didn't mix up the amounts, I had tucked the taxi money in my shirt pocket and folded two 1000-won notes—about $1.30 each—for the porters in my wallet.

Everything went according to the plan until I stepped up to pay for our lunch. As I began to search my wallet, I realized that I had mistakenly mixed up the two bills and had given the porters the 10,000-won notes that were supposed to pay for lunch (about $13.00 each). That generous tip may have made their day, but it didn't mine. I was so angry that I actually stomped my foot on the floor.

Greeted with curious stares from the folks lined up behind me, I began to realize how ridiculous it was for me to be upset. I was wasting a good deal more than $26 worth of adrenaline on the situation. I remembered a Visa card and paid for my meal, feeling very sheepish. My anger was the result of frustration with myself because I had made a mistake.

Failure to see your expectations met does the same thing. Failure in your marriage or in the lives of your children, failure to get the grade you deserved in a class at school, failure to receive the promotion you felt you deserved—all these and other such irritations produce frustration. When you have unrealistic expectations—ones that do not have a reasonable chance of being met, including goals that are unattainable—your frustration erupts in anger.

Says Dr. James Comer,

> People have a sense that the world is closing in on them, that there are too many people around and that they are getting ripped off. We feel powerless. All of a sudden, we're beginning to doubt that anybody can do anything about our problems, and we are angry. We explode in frustration.[3]

Large numbers of people today feel they are no longer in control, and they are seeing their dreams and aspirations for a better tomorrow evaporate. Ask them, "Are you better off today than you were five years ago?" and you will get a litany of negative answers. It is not simply the changes that have taken place since 9/11 and the emergence of terrorists who are so intent on taking your life that they are willing to sacrifice theirs. It is the world scene that promises little hope of peace in the future, the threat of global warming affecting the climate of the world, the crisis between the oil-producing nations and the oil consumers who are dependent on them (and consequently are angered by the inability of the government to either produce alternate sources of energy or control the accelerating prices confronting us).

It is not only in the U.S. that people feel like that. Large numbers of people who lived in the former U.S.S.R. greeted democracy with open arms, thinking it would give them what people often enjoy in the West, only to be deeply disappointed. It is not uncommon at all to hear things such as, "It was better under Communism because at least then we were guaranteed a job and bread." A retired military officer who had spent his life in the Ukrainian army said, "When I retired I could have bought two automobiles easily; now I can't buy two tires with the same money." Inflation had destroyed what he needed for the future. Of course he was angry.

Few of us can afford to deal with frustration as a friend of mine did. He took his trail bike into the mountains hunting. When it refused to run, John started tinkering with it, but it still wouldn't start. The longer he worked on it, the more he thought about missing his hunt and the madder he got. After enduring as much as his patience would stand, he drew his .45 pistol and proceeded to blast the bike into oblivion, then push it off a cliff and walk out. Sometimes we'd like to do something like that, but it just isn't economically feasible. Who hasn't at some time or another wanted to take a hammer to his computer when it failed to respond to his wishes?

Yes, you are angry at what's happening in our world today, but there is no particular person or thing that your anger is directed against—which is why it may seep out a bit every day or explode in a conflagration of pain.

3. Personal affronts produce anger. Somebody tells a Polish joke and you happen to have parents who were born in Warsaw; or they call you a "gringo" or a "Jap." You take it as an insult, and you allow your temper to flare.

One time I arrived in an African country where I was to speak, and having had enough of being cooped up on a plane, I was ready to get off as soon as we hit the ground. I was the first one out the door, and consequently the first person to arrive at customs.

I handed my passport to the customs officer, who lazily took it and started to process it, but when a couple of nationals arrived, he pushed my passport to the back of his desk and processed theirs first. I stood there and waited rather patiently, but each time a national approached my passport got shoved back farther, and I grew a little warmer under the collar. I had enough sense to realize I was a guest in the country, and so I kept my mouth shut and my emotions in hand, but it made me realize that personal injustice is one of the reasons why people allow their tempers to get out of control.

What I experienced was nothing compared to what some sustain over long periods of time, whether the affront is because of their faith, their ethnic background, their personal appearance, or whatever. You can't help becoming angry when you are targeted unjustly.

4. The violation of your rights produces anger. In marriage a man expects certain things of his wife, and she in turn also expects certain things of her husband. Those expectations—which often are not perceived the same way by a husband and wife—are usually the result of seeing certain things in the home in which a person grew up. When those expectations are not realized, or the rights and privileges that one of you extends to the other are not returned, irritation turns into anger.

We consider being slighted as an attack on our person, and we aren't going to sit there and let somebody walk over us, no sir! We're going to stand up for our rights (even if it blows a marriage apart)! You may win the argument, but lose a friend or possibly a spouse in the process.

Society today has become very conscious of what is perceived as a "right," and at times that perception means the individual feels an entitlement that neither God nor the constitution guarantees. Nonetheless, he or she becomes angry, and—whether it is a shooting on a college campus or a post-office worker who goes berserk and becomes violent with a supervisor—innocent people suffer.

5. Situations that counter your value system produce anger. A study of the life of Jesus indicates that most of His anger was occasioned by situations that were wrong, and He did something about them. Call it "righteous indignation," or whatever you like, but we need more of it.

Newspapers recently told of a woman driving down a street, when she saw two muggers rifling the pockets of a man who had his hands in the air. She stopped, figuring it was a holdup, and began to honk the horn of her car. This occasioned a blast of a 12-gauge shotgun at her car as the robbers made a getaway in their vehicle. But undaunted, the woman leaned on the horn of her car and trailed the suspects, who soon crashed into a parked car and were arrested by police. She told a reporter, "I just said to myself, I'm not going to let them get away with that! I guess I just got mad."

Learning to Cope with Anger

Though anger is potentially a negative emotion, and used improperly can create lots of havoc, used properly (as in the true story I just related) it works for our good and that of society in general. The following are five guidelines which you can use in learning to cope with anger in such a way that it take its rightful place in your life.

Guideline 1: Learn to cope with anger by avoiding stressful situations

to the extent that you can. Naturally, you can't avoid them all, but you can some. If you are going to fly, you know ahead of time that you are going to get hassled going through security. If your suitcase is substantially overweight, you know that you are going to be hit with a surcharge. If you—not your suitcase—are considerably overweight, be prepared to be asked by airline personnel to purchase two seats. No wonder people today are considering alternatives to flying.

To the degree that you can, organize yourself and your schedule so you eliminate pressured situations that evoke anger, like consistently getting up too late, which means you drive too fast to work; or failing to leave for the airport on time; or planning your time so tightly that the slightest change of schedule really angers you. Planning ahead can eliminate some of those situations that are apt to trigger your temper.

Perhaps it means changing churches rather than staying where you have been for the last 25 years and becoming bitter and angry. Perhaps it means going ahead and buying a new car instead of coping with the frustration of trying to keep a car running when it should have passed from the scene a long time ago. Perhaps it means changing jobs rather than staying where you have been bypassed for promotion. But of course there are those times when you can't change things and must, of necessity, pray that God will give you the grace to accept what you cannot change.

Not all stressful situations can be avoided, which means that additional coping skills have to be developed.

Guideline 2: Learn to cope with anger by putting the circumstances in perspective. When you start to feel the slow burn, stop and ask yourself, *Is the situation really worth the emotional stress and strain of getting angry?* You need to ask sometimes, *Is that person worth losing my temper over?* The problem with too many people today is that they are temperamental—too much temper and not enough mental.

Is it worth the risk of getting fired to tell your boss what you think of him? What does it do to your wife and children? And so what if I tipped the porters ten times the amount I intended! Life is going to go on, and a few days beyond the frustration, it won't matter. And besides, as my wife suggested, maybe God used that gift to meet a tremendous need in their lives! Who knows?

Put the circumstances into perspective and you'll learn that over the long haul, losing your temper isn't worth the frustration and the turmoil in your life it occasions.

Guideline 3: Learn to contain your anger if it threatens your welfare or that of others. Undisciplined anger takes its toll on your future success in the business world, your marriage and happiness, your parenting, and your body physically.

Let's start with what it does to your health:

- Research in the 1950s demonstrated that uncontrolled anger creates physical problems ranging "all the way from arthritis to asthma, from urinary disorders to the common cold," reports Dr. Leo Maddow in his book *Anger*.[4]

- "Women who don't let out their strong feelings—including anger—are at a higher risk of getting cancer," notes Josette Mondanaro, MD, director of a women's medical clinic.[5]

- "Anger in its rawest form is a physical response that causes a rise in blood pressure, constriction of the arterial vessels of the heart and the release of a hormone called noradrenalin [a hormone that researchers connect with anger]," says Peggy Eastman in an article entitled "I'm So Angry I Could Die!"[6]

- Recent findings of researchers who studied 1769 men and 1913 women show that hotheaded men—the tough guys who can't control their tempers—are at risk with heart disease in ways that seemingly do not affect women. Men with fiery tempers have a 10 percent greater risk of heart flutter (atrial fibrillation, if you prefer a more sophisticated term), which leads to strokes, which lead to the back door of the mortuary. Furthermore, men who are hostile—the kind who seem to walk around with a chip on their shoulder—are 30 percent more likely to develop heart disease, which also shortens their lives.

Then think how anger affects your circumstances. A study of corporate executives demonstrates that most have tempers, yet most of them know when to suppress them and when to vent them. Failing to know how and when to do that can cost you the success you desire in the business world or in the workplace. Take, for example, a young junior executive who worked for a bank. No one could deny he had the marks of a rising leader. He had a good educational background, a graduate degree in banking—good credentials—and he generally made good decisions. But he had one flaw. He couldn't hold his temper. When he didn't get his way, he exploded. Most of the time, people didn't push him. They stayed out of his way. But when the position of general manager became vacant, management passed over him and promoted a less qualified individual. Everybody knew he had better qualifications, but the other person could work with people.

> Far too often when we are bothered by something our responses are emotional overkill.

James, the half brother of Jesus, wrote, "My dear brothers, take note of this: Everyone should be quick to listen, slow to speak and slow to become angry" (James 1:19). Today we are slow to listen, quite ready to speak, and prone to anger. There are times, however, when the kingdom of God as well as your personal life is better served by your learning to discipline your speech and keep your temper under control.

I'm thinking of a Seattle father of three who was driving home at the end of a busy day when a car cut in front of him. Angered, he accelerated and passed the car, cutting in front of him, just as the other driver had done. Now both drivers were angry, and the one who initiated the exchange, pulled his car alongside the father of three, took a gun from beneath the seat, and pulled the trigger, killing the man instantly.

He vented his temper, but at great cost! When someone annoys you and you feel the ire rising within, you've got to ask yourself, "Is this guy worth it? Am I willing to stoop to his or her level?" You've got to remind yourself of the fact that you are wasting an awful lot of adrenaline over an issue that just isn't worth it. Far too often when we are bothered by something our responses are emotional overkill. It's like shooting a fly with a .45 instead of using a fly swatter. Far too much emotional energy is expended.

At times we need to be more like the father of a three-year-old who was shopping with his son in a department store. The dad would make comments such as, "Easy, Albert!" "Slow down, boy." "Get a handle on yourself, ol' buddy." A bystander overheard the father and said, "I'm a child psychologist, and I'd like to commend you on the way you handle your son, little Albert here."

"My son, nothing!" replied the man. "*My* name is Albert!"

Guideline 4: Vent your emotions so anger doesn't breed in your heart. When you become angry, you have basically three options:

- *deny your anger* (which is obvious to almost everyone except you)

- *suppress your anger*—stuff it inside (while you are still angry), storing and cataloging grievances and annoyances)

- *vent your anger in a proper manner*

Individuals who deny they are angry are playing mind games with themselves. I am thinking of a conversation that was overheard as a woman and her friend were in a restaurant. The woman was describing the failures of her husband.

"You're angry with him, aren't you?" said the friend.

"I am not angry," she retorted.

Her friend followed this by, "Well, then why are you shouting at me?"

Though there is a time and a place for anger, generally displays of anger in public are more apt to make people uncomfortable and perhaps create a situation you can't handle.

Now, meet three people who mishandle their anger:

- First, meet "Peace-at-any-price Polly." Polly grew up in a home with an alcoholic father, whose outbursts of temper produced beatings and foul language. She learned not to trigger his temper, but when she did, she felt guilty. Although she said she would never marry anyone like her dad, she did that very thing, and when her husband developed a drinking problem, she suppressed her anger.

- The second individual who suppresses anger is "Mabel the

Manipulator." She has a hard time saying what's on her mind, so when communication is difficult she fights back with mood swings, headaches, and pouting. Actually, she is a world-class manipulator, who browbeats her husband into letting her have her way. She's angry and she doesn't know how to handle it properly.

- The third person I'd like to describe is "Sam the Sacker." Sam keeps a large emotional gunnysack handy, and when people anger him, he stays fairly cool on the outside, but he makes a careful note of his injustice and stores it away. Eventually he dumps the sack of emotional garbage on someone, going back into the past and documenting every injustice he has received.

All three of these individuals are angry, yet they would deny it. Dr. Paul Carlson, a Christian psychiatrist and a man I highly respect, has written,

> Anger, in my opinion, is like energy. It cannot be destroyed, but it can be stored or its form can be changed. When we bury the anger within us and repeatedly deny its existence, it accumulates in what I have chosen to call an unresolved anger fund. The more we suppress anger, the more it accumulates.

Venting your anger can be done properly (the subject of the next section). You can do it in such a manner that you are not embarrassed afterward, nor does your display of anger hurt others or bring reproach and shame upon yourself and the cause of Christ.

Does that mean that when your ire is rising, you are entitled to just cut loose, get it out of your system, and say whatever makes you feel good? No! Research clearly proves that emotional outbursts are counterproductive to you as well as to the object of your wrath, in spite of the common belief to the contrary.

When David Wilkerson was working among street gangs in New York City, he was taken through a primary school in a troubled area. When he noticed a classroom where the teacher was absent, and the youngsters, about age eight, were frolicking and cavorting around, generally out of control, he asked, "What's going on here?" He was told that this was "expression time" when the teacher vacated the room for a few minutes allowing the youngsters to express themselves and vent their emotions.

In the 1960s and 1970s some psychologists thought that the way to get anger out of your system was to cut loose with a so-called primal scream. (Who ever thought up the idea that our ancestors stood in a field and yelled or screamed uncontrollably?) Or else, troubled individuals should closet themselves with other angry individuals and utter profanities and expletives at whatever annoyed them. Research, however, has demonstrated that "getting it out of your system" doesn't remove the root of bitterness and anger, and produces no lasting relief whatsoever.

Guideline 5: Learn to cope with anger by eliminating stressful situations. This guideline, of necessity, will not apply to everything that disturbs you, but if there is a situation that constantly irritates you and you *can* do something about it, then *do* it. When you consistently leave a worship service at your church grim and annoyed—even angry—perhaps it's time to change churches if you can't change the things about your church that make you angry.

Perhaps it means going ahead and buying a new car instead of coping with the frustration of trying to keep that gas guzzler away from the pump and being angry about the cost of fuel.

But of course there are those times when you can't change things and must, of necessity, pray that God will give you the grace to accept what you cannot change.

This section contains guidelines that will help you learn how to be "good and mad" without being bad! They are based on Paul's direction to the Ephesians: "Be ye angry, and sin not: let not the sun go down upon your wrath" (Ephesians 4:26 KJV).

How to Make Anger Work *for* You

Guideline 1: Be angry with the right person. Too often we take out hostility on the wrong person—usually an innocent one who happens to be in the wrong place at the wrong time. Like this situation: You are really angry with your boss, but not having the courage to confront him, you come home all hot under the collar. When you get to the garage, you notice that your son's bicycle is not in its proper place and you instinctively yell at him. Sure, you told him at least a dozen times to put his bike away when he finishes riding, but the intensity of your feelings goes way beyond the seriousness of the situation.

Misplaced aggression is one of the prime reasons for child abuse and physical violence among adults. Being unable to handle anger on the job, we vent the feelings on weak and helpless victims who generally can't or won't fight back.

This is why Jesus instructed us to go to the person with whom we have a problem and deal with the problem one to one (see Matthew 18:15 and following). This way you allow your anger to be dispelled in a right way with the right person.

When two of our daughters were helping to defray college expenses by waiting tables at a local restaurant, often people who would never have the courage to tell the manager they thought the prices were too high, or the air conditioning was inadequate, would take out their annoyances on them. Anger, misplaced, is never constructive.

Guideline 2: Be angry for the right cause. Part of our problem today is that we are angry over the wrong causes. What should evoke "moral indignation" or old-fashioned anger is met with indifference, and what angers us should be met with discipline and tact. There is a time and a place for anger, as Ecclesiastes 3:1-8 states.

Jesus gave us an example when He became angry with the money changers who had turned the temple into a den of merchandise:

> Jesus entered the temple area and drove out all who were buying and selling there. He overturned the tables of the moneychangers and the benches of those selling doves. "It is written," he said to them, "'My house will be called a house of prayer,' but you are making it a 'den of robbers'" (Matthew 21:12-13).

Jesus was angry, and rightly so! We need to get angry at the inroads of pornography, indecency in public life, corruption in government, and such issues today—at least as angry as we become when our favorite television program is pre-empted by a football game we're not interested in watching.

Guideline 3: Be angry for the right duration of time. That's the sum of Paul's advice "Don't let the sun go down on your wrath." His advice is to get it out of your system. Say it as kindly as possible, but get it off your chest. Don't carry it over to the next day.

In his book *Under His Wing*, Bernie May describes "the R & R response," or the time it takes you to go from *reaction* to *recovery*. He believes your maturity can well be measured by the amount of time it takes you to transition from the pain of reaction to the healing of recovery. He quotes an anonymous source as saying, "You are young only once, but you can be immature for a lifetime." Right!

Now, how does this apply to your life today? First, focus on something that happened to you recently, something unpleasant that you did not plan and certainly would have avoided if you could have. This is probably not too difficult. Can you identify with these?

- *Item 1:* Your wife drove the family car after the radiator hose had broken, and consequently, the engine block cracked. In your superior wisdom you knew that a car should not be driven without radiator fluid. Anybody should have that much sense, you loudly announced when you heard about it. You were just as steamed as the radiator.

- *Item 2:* You said something about a fellow employee at the fax machine. It wasn't malicious, and you didn't intend to hurt anyone, but the office busybody overhead you and embellished what you said, putting it in a different context and repeating it to the person involved, who confronted you. Now you have an enemy.

- *Item 3:* Your pen at the office—the one with your name on it—constantly ends up in the desk drawer of another person. You say he steals it—he says he borrows it.

How long does it take for you to recover when you have been wronged? A few minutes, a few days or months, or perhaps even years? That time or distance between reaction and response is a pretty good measure of your emotional and spiritual maturity.

Some people never recover. The rest of their life is spent in reaction—

angry, bitter, unforgiving reaction. I shall never forget the man who sat in my office in Manila shortly after we moved there in 1974. He presented me with a legal file about two inches thick. He was angry. His eyes narrowed and his voice tensed as he told me of being fired—without cause, according to him—from his job. "And when did this happen?" I asked. "Twelve years ago," he responded.

All right, you got fired—perhaps without real cause; or your husband walked out on you and broke up your marriage; or someone threw eggs on your house and scribbled a hostile, racial message on your door. You reacted, of course. Whenever a nail gets driven into your heart or your hand, you react; but how long does it take you to cry out, "Father, forgive them, for they know not what they do"? That's the measure of your maturity as a Christian.

Those who hold on to wrong, living for revenge or demanding restitution, are the losers. They are living in a prison of hate, but those who say, "Okay, this happened, but I'm going to get on with my life," are the ones who find the grace of God to put something behind—which is what forgiveness is about. They are the real winners. If you want to outlive your enemies, get on with your life, forget they are enemies, ask God to help you forgive them, and release the bitterness from the past. That's how you move from reaction to recovery.

Guideline 4: Be angry in the right way. If anger can be directed against the problem rather than the person who has created the problem, it becomes constructive and positive. But when you put your fist through the wall or punch your brother-in-law who owes you money, you have only created a worse problem—not only your wallet hurts, but your fist will hurt the next day. Jesus was angry in the right way. He did something constructive—He eliminated the money changers from the temple. And you will find that usually those who are wrong will back down and flee, just as Jesus' adversaries did when He drove them from the temple.

When I was a student in college, there was a rule: "Constructive criticism is appreciated, but griping is not tolerated." Anger used properly can be a force that rights wrongs and corrects injustices, but used in the wrong way, leaves innocent victims hurt and distraught. When you are angry over a situation, ask, "Where should my anger be directed?"

Guideline 5: Live, love, and laugh. Once you have processed your anger, you can make the conscious decision to put it aside and refuse to become its captive. Although you may not make a conscious decision to be angry, you can make the decision to work through it, as I have outlined, then get on with your life.

Ingrid Betancourt did that following her captivity among FARC guerrillas in Colombia. Upon her release, after almost seven years of what she described as "hell," Larry King, the popular talk show host, interviewed her. "Do you hate them?" he asked her. She quickly responded, saying that when she was taken captive, she made the conscious decision not to hate her captors. Instead she clung to her faith in God and the hope she would once again be united with her children, whom she dearly loved. She knew that hatred consumes the heart and leaves little room for love or laughter.

While there is little to laugh about in a Colombian jungle where you are deprived of your freedom, learning to laugh displaces anger and hatred and gives you emotional strength.

Yes, there is a time and a place for everything, and by following these guidelines you will discover that something able to destroy your marriage or your job can work for you. With God's help, you can make anger your friend. As Ecclesiastes 3:1 says, "There is a time for everything, and a season for every activity under heaven," including times to be good—and mad—yes, both!

QUESTIONS FOR THOUGHT AND DISCUSSION

You are driving home on the freeway at the end of the day, when a smart aleck in a beat-up van cuts in front of you, forcing you to slam on your brakes or rear-end him. You lean on your horn, expressing your feelings, and the offending driver turns around and gives you the finger.

1. Name two times you have been angry recently. How did you cope with anger in each case? Was one situation easier to resolve than the other? If so, what did you do differently in that case?

2. Name an everyday situation about which you are angry regularly. What are some steps you can take to cope with that anger?

3. Name one situation about which you have been angry for a long time. Are you angry with the right person? Are you angry at the right cause? Has your anger lasted too long, considering the situation? Are you being angry in the right way? What are some positive ways you can work to resolve that anger?

This Will Hurt...

Many times, our natural reaction when we are offended or insulted is to try to put the other person in his place. We might want to step on the accelerator, zip around the guy in the van, and cut him off. If we can make solid eye contact with a fuming glare as we pass, we feel even more vindicated. All this really does for us, though, is to make us angrier and cause more stress. It will hurt if we keep thinking about the situation, tell people about it all day, or add it to our list of things that have gone wrong in life.

This Will Help...

An old proverb says, "He who overcomes another is strong, but he who overcomes himself is mighty!" It will help to take a deep breath and give yourself time to think about the situation. It will help to think through the guidelines given in this chapter about coping with anger. It is possible to lose your time, your energy, even your life over things that are not worth it.

The following suggestions may help you vent your emotions in positive ways:

- Get physical—run the stress out of your system by jogging, swimming, calisthenics, walking, or whatever.

- Do it through music. Leonard Bernstein once said, "It's a remarkably lucky thing to be able to storm your way through a Beethoven symphony. Think of the amount of rage you can get out. If you exhibited that on the streets or in an interpersonal relationship, you'd be thrown in jail. Instead, you're applauded for it." Better to beat a drum or the keyboard of a piano than be tempted to beat your kids or your wife.

- Do it through painting—transfer bursts of emotion to canvas rather than to the members of your family.

- Do it through prayer, as I suggested in the chapter on emotions and how to handle them.

Chapter 7

The Inner Struggle of Worry

Lyndon Johnson, the thirty-sixth president of the United States, once asked an elderly lady how she was getting along, and she replied, "Fine!" She explained:

> When I walks, I walks slowly,
> When I sits, I sits loosely.
> When I sees a worry coming on me,
> I just lies down and goes to sleep.

Not everyone, however, is capable of doing that. I received a letter that expresses a common struggle Christians have: "I'm a Christian, and I know I shouldn't worry, but I do. Is there anything I can do to overcome this?" Indeed, there is! That's what this chapter is about.

I confess I occasionally catch myself worrying about nonsensical things. Of course, I know better. So what qualifies me to even include a chapter on this topic? Experience—the negative kind, as one who has been there and done his fair share of worrying, but also as one who has also learned through experience that there is a better, more satisfying way. Jesus told the disciples quite bluntly, "Don't worry about your life!"

I've also found that if we are to cast our burdens on the Lord, as the psalmist instructs, and to cast our every care on the Lord, as Peter tells us we ought to do, then either God is asking us to do the impossible (something He never does), or else this is something we can and must learn to do!

What I'm sharing with you in this chapter is part of my spiritual journey over more than a few years. Frankly, I've written and rewritten this chapter several times. As I've tossed pages into the recycle bin (a.k.a. trash can) commenting, "Too simplistic!" or "Trite," I've started rewriting, striving to be realistic and yet optimistic. We can live above the flood tide of worry that engulfs so many—not with a syrupy religiosity that is a veneer for hypocrisy but with a simple faith that engages our Father's care and concern for our lives, striving to recapture childlike trust in Him. Okay, let's get started.

It seems that nearly everybody worries about something these days. We worry about the weather, the purity of the water we drink, our health, global warming, or what may happen in the world. We worry about Israel's dropping "the bomb" on Syria, or what Iran may do to precipitate a crisis of gargantuan proportions in the Middle East. We worry about terrorism, rising prices, and shrinking bank accounts. Single folks worry about getting married, and some of the married folks I know worry about staying that way.

Even kids are getting in on the worry game, according to psychologists, who say that it is nothing unusual for ten-year-olds to show up with ulcers because of the social and home pressures they are under. Whether you are eight or eighty, your body will keep score when you worry. It's the way God made you. Inevitably, your body becomes tense, muscles tighten, and

> Worry has become a growing industry... Thousands of people have bought into a variety of cures.

you feel its deadly result. I have never seen an obituary that read, "So and so died of worry!" But hypertension, heartburn, angina, high blood pressure, and a host of other maladies are the results of worry.

On one occasion a doctor took the blood pressure of a dignified, cultured woman and couldn't believe how high it was. "What's going on in your life right now?" asked her physician. "I can explain," she said, somewhat miffed, adding, "I just had an argument with someone in the waiting room, and I guess that's the result of it."

Worry has become a growing industry. Our inability to cope with worry sends us to psychiatrists, psychologists, therapists, and counselors as well as to the pharmacy to help quiet the troubled waters of our lives. Searching for an answer to the problem, thousands of people have bought into a variety of cures—from pop psychology and New Age teaching to self-help books. Today there is a wide spectrum of proposed solutions, from cults to Bible-oriented teaching.

Worry Among Believers

One of the strange things about worry is that it seems to have as many professing Christians as nonbelievers among its victims. How many Christians do you know who are known for their smooth brow and calmness of temperament?

Now, of course, if there is no God who controls the affairs of your life, then you had better worry about the future; the success or failure of your life hinges on your efforts alone! But on the other hand, if there is a God in heaven who will direct and guide you, if there is a God who hears and answers your prayers, then you waste your time and dissipate a tremendous amount of energy when you worry. Yes, I know you believe that but still catch yourself occasionally with wrinkled brow and irritated demeanor.

The Bible addresses this issue head-on. Take the time to look up the references to anxiety or worry in a concordance. Most of the passages you'll find listed there are from one of two primary spokesmen: Jesus and the apostle Paul. Jesus said more about worry than all the other writers of Scripture put together.

Among the issues He addresses are what we are going to eat or drink, and what we will wear (see Matthew 6:25-34). His followers should not worry about what to say when they are brought into conflict with government authorities (see Matthew 10:19). He told Martha that she was "worried and upset about many things" (Luke 10:41), but that those things were not worth the stress they created.

But it was Paul, the second most vocal spokesman, who clarified the difference between *worry* and *concern*. Concern, Paul taught, is legitimate. Concern for your health or physical safety, or concern for people may motivate you to take steps necessary for well-being. Worry, on the other hand, is the persistent, nagging, debilitating concern over something you can generally do nothing about.

Part of the reason it is hard to distinguish between the two is that the line between concern and worry is very fine. Paul says that an unmarried man is *concerned*—the same word usually translated as *worry*—about the Lord's work, whereas a married person is concerned about pleasing his or her mate (1 Corinthians 7:32-34). The body of Christ is to show concern, but not worry, for each other (1 Corinthians 12:25). Concern should be a positive force resulting in our enrichment and betterment.

Now, let's read beyond the headline and notice some of the fine print of what Jesus and Paul said about worry. In the Sermon on the Mount, Jesus said,

> I tell you, do not worry about your life, what you will eat or drink; or about your body, what you will wear. Is not life more important than food, and the body more important than clothes? (Matthew 6:25).

Then I can just see Jesus gesture toward the birds that were flitting over the fields surrounding Galilee as He said,

> Look at the birds of the air; they do not sow or reap or store away in barns, and yet your heavenly Father feeds them. Are you not much more valuable than they? (Matthew 6:26).

Worry is completely needless, Jesus said—a conviction few of us have today. Worry accomplishes nothing positive. Instead, it deprives us of needed sleep. It dissipates our energy and leaves us weary. Like a broken record that plays the same scratchy track over and over again, worry occupies our minds with unproductive thoughts. It keeps us from seeking out productive solutions, and it never changes anything.

Worry Is Needless Because of God's Care for Us

Immediately before His death and resurrection, Jesus met with His disciples in the Upper Room. There He gave them what could be considered His last instructions regarding the future. He said, "Stop letting your hearts be troubled [and that spells worry]. You believe in God, believe also in me" (John 14:1, author's translation). The message in all Scripture is that worry is needless because there is a God in heaven who is fully in control of the situation and has demonstrated a personal concern for your life.

Paul focused in on this universal problem of worry when he wrote these words to the Philippians:

> Don't worry about anything; instead, pray about everything; tell God your needs, and don't forget to thank him for his answers. If you do this, you will experience God's peace, which is far more wonderful than the human mind can understand. His peace will keep your thoughts and your hearts quiet and at rest as you trust in Christ Jesus (Philippians 4: 6-7 TLB).

Paul's antidote is simple: "Don't worry about anything—pray about everything." This means, quite simply put, that you can take the everyday needs of your life to God and trust Him for a solution. A mother who is concerned about the social adjustment of her six year old can make this a matter of prayer rather than worry about it. A father who is concerned about the possibility of his job running out, which means unemployment and insufficient income for the family, can make this a matter of prayer rather than debilitating anxiety. A teenager who is waiting to hear about being accepted into college can trust God rather than worry.

By its very nature, worry says you don't believe God is big enough, or powerful enough, or willing enough to do anything about the needs of your life; therefore, you yourself had better be concerned. When you find yourself worrying, ask yourself if that's what you actually believe.

Worry Is Needless Because of the Providence of God

I believe it was primarily because of God's faithful provision that Jesus was so hard on those who worry. And if He were here today, He wouldn't smile gently and say, "You can't help it, I know. Life is tough in the twenty-first century." He knew that God is all-powerful, and He understood that our heavenly Father is honor-bound to keep His word. The law and the prophets clearly teach that about God—a truth the disciples should have known. Moses wrote, "God is not a man, that he should lie, nor a son of man, that he should change his mind. Does he speak and then not act? Does he promise and not fulfill?" (Numbers 23:19).

Simply put, Jesus believed that God would fulfill His responsibility to His children; therefore, the relationship of a son with the Father should be that of trust, not fear or even duty. Mark records the prayer of Jesus from the Garden of Gethsemane: "Abba, Father...everything is possible for you. Take this cup from me. Yet not what I will, but what you will" (Mark 14:35).

The fact that God has a will for you that goes far beyond your limited vision and understanding is part of a great truth we call the providence of God. It is embodied in Proverbs 3:5-6, where we find these words:

> Trust in the LORD with all your heart and lean not on your
> own understanding; in all your ways acknowledge him, and
> he will make your paths straight.

Those last words, "He will make your paths straight," are God's promise of guidance no matter how limited your understanding or how dark the world in which you live.

When I think of God's providential guidance, I think of Joseph, who was sold into slavery by his own brothers. It was a dreadful situation that appeared to be hopeless from a human perspective. Then, from the lowly position of a slave, Joseph was elevated to prime minister. And Joseph could say to his brothers, "You intended to harm me, but God intended it for good" (Genesis 50:20).

When things go wrong in your life, do you have that assurance? When you have more bills than you have money, or illness strikes in your family, do you have the deep-settled confidence that God works all things after the counsel of His own will, as Paul tells us in Ephesians 1:11?

This doesn't mean that you will never face money problems. It is a promise, however, that those problems will not overwhelm you. It doesn't mean that you will not face personal problems or difficulties. But it does mean that you need not be crushed by them. It means that God will be with you as you face the battles of life.

Worry Is Futile

Jesus indicated worry's futility by asking, "Who of you by worrying can add a single hour to his life?" (Matthew 6:27). The obvious answer to that question is, "None of us!" His point was, however, that your life is of concern to your heavenly Father. Then Jesus mentions something that in modern days we have come to appreciate in a new way. He says, "Even the very hairs of your head are all numbered. So don't be afraid; you are worth more than many sparrows" (Matthew 10:30-31).

A speaking trip to Washington, DC, gave me a few hours for sightseeing. Like most men—little boys at heart—I was interested in visiting the FBI Building. Over the years the Federal Bureau of Investigation has had a worldwide reputation for being one of the most thorough crime investigation groups in existence. I was especially interested in their laboratory analyses—such as how DNA works and how a criminal could be identified with very little to work with. Expert technicians take a shred—perhaps a few threads—of fabric, a chip of paint, a tiny chip of metal, or what have you, and reconstruct a compelling case for what happened.

One agent said that from a single strand of hair, chemists can tell whether it was cut, fell out, or was pulled from the scalp. If it was cut, they can tell whether the instrument was sharp, dull, scissors, a knife, or cut with an improvised tool such as a shard of glass. They can tell whether the hair had been bleached, dyed, given a permanent, or otherwise changed, whether the person was healthy or sickly, whether or not he had taken drugs, and if so, what kind. All of that information, plus a great deal more. Think about this. The English poet John Keats had been dead for 166 years when chemists analyzed a lock of his hair and concluded that he had taken large doses of morphine because of his terminal tuberculosis.

If God has the very hairs of your head numbered (something that has become easier and easier for Him to do with me as I've grown older) and something as insignificant as this is of concern to Him, why should we worry? "Are you not worth more than many sparrows?" He asks.

A soldier who determined that worry wouldn't get the best of him carried the following on a little card in his helmet:

> One of two things is certain. Either you are at the front or else behind the lines. If at the front, of two things one is certain. Either you are exposed to danger or in a safe place. If exposed to danger, of two things, one is certain, you are either wounded or not. If wounded, you will either recover or die. IF YOU DIE, YOU CAN'T WORRY...SO WHY WORRY NOW?

That soldier had wisely come to recognize the futility of worry!

Worry is unrealistic. Most of the things we worry about never materialize. That was confirmed by the findings of a panel of psychologists who met together to study the effects of worry. They concluded that 40 percent of what we worry about never happens. Then, 30 percent of our worries are about past events—things that have already happened, which cannot be changed, such as how well you did on last Friday's test or in the sales presentation you made last week. Another 12 percent of our worries are needless health concerns—the "what-ifs."[1] I know one woman who majored on those concerns. She said she always felt bad when she felt good because she knew she would eventually feel bad again. She did...eventually!

Then, about 10 percent of our worries involve trifling things of absolutely no consequence. Only 8 percent of our worries, according to the research of that panel of psychologists, are valid areas of concern. As Mark Twain wisely observed, "I am an old man and have known a great many troubles, but most of them never happened!"

We have lost sight of the great truth of God's providence and His care for His children. We quote Romans 8:28—"We know that in all things God works for the good of those who love him"—while at the same time we allow our stomachs to knot and we worry about the very things we have not bothered to pray about. Heartburn becomes the badge of our faith, and Maalox becomes the wine of our defunct communion with God.

George Lyons was right when he wrote, "Worry is the interest paid by those who borrow trouble." The senseless thing about worry is that it does nothing to change the future or what might—but probably will not—happen. What it does is effectively neutralize our productivity today.

Worry vs. concern. Worry, which is the persistent refusal to do something about something except to allow it to destroy your peace of mind, is different from concern over an issue that causes you to take action. One of the defense mechanisms God gave us for our own protection is legitimate concern. For example, if cancer runs in your family, then follow your doctor's advice regarding diet and medical care. If something appears that you feel is abnormal, that concern should prompt you to see a doctor immediately. Worry, however, is living as though you are doomed by the concern you refuse to face. Concern over your health may prompt you to get a checkup from your doctor; worry, however, paralyzes you.

May I be very candid and frank? If you are in basic agreement with this point, if you recognize that worry is futile and useless because of God's care and His concern for your life, and yet you worry, call it what it actually is—*sin*. "Anyone…who knows the good he ought to do and doesn't do it, sins" (James 4:17). And no sin—whether it is socially acceptable or not—is acceptable in God's sight.

Some people will protest, "But I can't help worrying; it's my nature!" There is no scientific evidence that worry is a part of anyone's nature. However, Dr. Paul Carlson, a Christian psychiatrist, believes that some individuals are *more prone* to worry than others by virtue of their emotional and psychological makeup. Just as some have stronger vision than others and some are capable of physical feats far beyond the average, it can only follow that some are more trusting than others and less prone to worry. Whatever our makeup, the vast majority of the time we choose to worry because we are uncertain we can really trust God.

To the extent you can do something about worry, God holds you responsible. Let's face it—you can worry as though there is no God in heaven, or you can determine to trust Him to do what He knows best. Only He can do that. Maybe you are so close to the problem that you have lost sight of God's magnitude and true greatness. Perhaps you have never learned the elementary lesson that He is sufficient and powerful enough to handle any situation.

God never intended you to be a prisoner of fear or worry. As Martin Luther once said about temptation, you may not be able to prevent the birds from flying overhead, but you definitely can keep them from building a nest in your hair.

How to Beat the Habit

The following are some practical guidelines that will help you turn worry into trust.

Guideline 1: Acknowledge that worry has become a problem. If there were an organization called Worriers Anonymous, those who attend the meetings would have to introduce themselves by saying something like, "My name is John Doe, and I'm a worrier!" Admitting that worry has become chronic is the first step toward a long-term solution to the problem.

You may think, *I can handle my problems. Sure, I do a little bit of worrying—everybody does—but I don't need any help.* A lot of people cannot handle their problems, and they beat a path to the doors of psychiatrists and counselors. Perhaps you are one of those rugged individualists who can handle them. But on the other hand, how wise is it for you to carry the burden of worry when God says that you should not? There is a solution—entrust that concern to Him.

Picture a man at the side of the highway with a tremendous pack on his back. He can barely walk under its heavy load as he makes his way slowly toward the city. Then, an empty flatbed truck comes along. The driver, seeing the weariness of the man, pulls over and says, "Hey, buddy, put your load on the truck bed. I'll take you to town." We'd wonder at the first man's sanity if he said, "No, thanks—I can handle my burdens without your help."

Now, suppose the man with the pack does get up on the back of the empty truck, but he refuses to take the pack off even though he is now riding on the back of the truck. You'd probably doubt his sanity even more, right?

When a believer worries, he is like the man on the flatbed truck. He could lay his burden down and let the strength of the vehicle move it for him. Christ has paid the price for your burden, and He has indicated His willingness to bear your load if you will entrust it to Him. The first step is to acknowledge that worry has become a problem, and that He is the only one who can do anything about it: "He himself bore our sins [including what worries you] in his body on the tree" (1 Peter 2:24).

This is not something you do once in a lifetime; rather, it is something you have to do every time you find yourself in the clutches of a new challenge, problem, or difficulty.

Guideline 2: Ask God in simple faith to deal with your problem. Remember Paul's advice? "Don't worry about anything; pray about everything!" Today we seem to do the reverse—we worry about almost everything and pray about practically nothing. God's psychiatry begins with trust; be specific and ask Him to deal with the problem that kept you turning and tossing last night. Ask Him to come to your aid and remove that nagging thought.

> You need to speak very plainly to God. Remember, He knows exactly what is driving you to the brink.

Corrie ten Boom was a woman who, in her day, had plenty to worry about. During World War 2, Corrie, along with her father and her sister, Betsie, was arrested by the Gestapo at their home in Haarlem in the Netherlands. Her father died a week after he was arrested. Betsie died in the Ravensbruck concentration camp, and though Corrie's execution was scheduled, she was released the week before it by a fluke—no, by God's sovereign direction.

In her book *Each New Day* Corrie writes,

> When I worry I go to the mirror and say to myself, "This tremendous thing which is worrying me is beyond a solution. It is especially too hard for Jesus Christ to handle." After I have said that, I smile and I am ashamed.

It is at this point, however, you need to speak very plainly to God. Remember, He knows exactly what is driving you to the brink—feelings of loneliness, weakness, and estrangement. Pray, "Lord, You know how I feel right now. I know I should not worry but right now I can't help it. Please, Father, take charge of this situation. It is way beyond my grasp to do anything about. Lord, I don't want to get in the way of Your solution so I'm going to wait quietly on You."

Then, take the most difficult step yet.

Guideline 3: Act in obedience to the Word of God in this matter. The Bible says that worries are to be cast upon a Savior who cares. Peter wrote, "Cast all your anxiety on him because he cares for you" (1 Peter 5:7). What beautiful words for a world filled with cutthroat competition, a world seemingly so cold and friendless. Psalm 55:22 has similar words of advice: "Cast your burden upon the LORD, and He will sustain you" (NASB).

Never shall I read these two verses without vividly remembering a 4:30 a.m. encounter with them. Here's how it happened. I had bought a new stereo system, and as I was trying to dislodge the speaker which was stuck in the Styrofoam packing, I gave it a tug. But it was something in my back—not the shipping box—that broke loose.

The next day my back was sore but I could navigate. The following day my wife and I were scheduled to leave for ministry in Siberia, which meant flying to Seoul, Korea, then Khabarovsk, Russia, then on to Yakutsk—a rather long journey. When I woke, I could not walk without quite severe pain that started in my back and worked down my leg. I paced the floor, thinking, *I can walk this off,* and I prayed, *Lord, should I go or not go?* Getting Russian visas and transportation had been no small challenge.

No, I did not hear a voice that morning, but the words of Peter leaped into my memory:

> Humble yourselves, therefore, under God's mighty hand, that he may lift you up in due time. Cast all your anxiety on him because he cares for you (1 Peter 5:6-7).

As I thought about the situation, I told myself, *You are going to hurt no matter where you are, so you might as well go and trust God.* I did! Would I make the same decision again? Yes, I would. I put into practice what I'm telling you to do. Easy? No! Something I "felt" like doing? Again, negative. The easiest thing would have been to have cancelled the whole trip and sought medical help (which I can assure you I did the day following my return to the U.S.). But trusting God to do what we cannot do for ourselves is what the next guideline is about.

Guideline 4: Commit to Him what He alone can do. To put God's psychiatry into action requires something fundamental and very difficult: commitment. You need to come to the place where you can say, "I refuse to worry about this. I'm going to turn it over to the Lord and let Him deal with it." Many if not most of the issues that keep us awake at night, tossing and turning, are things that only God can change. But it is our nature to *fix* things, and when we can't, we worry about it.

A friend of mine tells of an acquaintance who was mountain climbing. A piton—a spike driven into the face of the rock to support a rope— didn't hold, and he had the sickening sensation he was going to fall. He only hoped against hope that the piton below that one would hold. Sure enough, he fell—and then, after what seemed like an eternity, the rope grew taut and held! Though dangling precariously from the end of a rope, he was alive. The measure of the man was that, though his forehead broke out in an icy sweat, he did not panic. But he dared not look down, and he kept thinking, *What if that one lone piton pulls out?*

He endured several excruciating minutes of agony and worry until his companions reached him. Only when they finally secured him would he allow himself to look below—and to his great surprise, he saw that less than three feet beneath him was a ledge wide enough to have easily supported him. Sometimes we needlessly hang on to our worries, not realizing that underneath are the everlasting arms of God (Deuteronomy 33:27). If you only could see God's hand of protection, how foolish your concerns would seem.

If you are the kind of person who internalizes thing—stuffs them inside, often hiding them from other people—you need to externalize your emotions and feelings in prayer, telling God exactly how you feel and what concerns you, going into detail as to why you are distressed. Doesn't He already know this? Of course, yet there is a freedom in expressing those emotions and feelings. Did Jesus not do exactly the same thing in the Garden of Gethsemane as He prostrated Himself before the Father and poured out His heart? Yes, He did. God does not hit us over the head or rebuke His children who vent their emotions in prayer. He knows and is compassionate. And as you release your pent-up emotions in prayer, letting the tears flow, you will discover the comfort of the Holy Spirit in a way that brings peace to your troubled heart.

Guideline 5: Refuse to worry, and worry, and keep on worrying over the same issue. Once you have committed your worry to the Lord as best as you know how, you can make the conscious decision that you are going to leave the problem with Him and not take it up again the next morning where you left off the night before. This is a choice you consciously make! When you awaken the next morning and catch yourself mentally replaying the concern that drove you to your knees the day before, you have to say, "Lord, we talked about this yesterday, and I now find myself starting to worry again. Would you please work it out without my help?"

If you catch yourself waking in the night, concerned about the same situation, pray, "Lord, I refuse to stay awake and be concerned about this. You take over the night shift—no sense in both of us staying awake."

When I do what I've just told you to do, I then begin to quote Scripture back to the Lord—one of the surest ways to fall asleep. (Memorize some of the verses I've quoted on worry.) My wife flips on her MP3 player and listens to music that allows her to focus on God instead of what concerns her.

Think His thoughts. Realize that if you could only see what worries you from His perspective, there would be no concern whatsoever.

There is one more thing, however, that needs to be said. Once you have taken step five, you aren't finished. There have been times when I have had to take that step more than once. Thinking I had really committed something to the Lord, I later found myself—usually when I was tired physically—starting to feel concern again, just as I had when I first put the issue in the Lord's hands, saying, "Lord, I can't handle this—You take it over!"

Guideline 6: Refocus on the Father and let His peace fill your heart. Worry has been called "the acceptable sin of the saints." Even so, it is not God's purpose or pleasure to see His children so loaded with cares. When you are prone to worry, listen quietly and you will hear the faint echo of His words spoken to men and women long ago: "Do not be afraid, little flock, for your Father has been pleased to give you the kingdom" (Luke 12:32). There can be no kingdom without a king, and when you are convinced that Jesus is Lord, it should be easier to focus on Him who will return as King of kings and Lord of lords and to refuse to buy into the mentality that everything depends on you.

When you set your focus on "things above," the "things below" are far less distracting. Concerned? Of course you will be. That's life lived out in a broken world. But you are not controlled by what creases the brows of those who are not children of the King.

In his book *Questions Jesus Asked,* Clovis Chappell told the story of a pilot who, in the early days of aviation, was attempting to fly around the world. At one remote place, he filled his plane with fuel and took off. Suddenly he noticed a gnawing sound. *What's that?* he thought, his brain running through a mental checklist. Suddenly it hit him: "That's the gnawing of a rat that must have slipped into the cockpit when the door was open back there!"

What to do, was the question. He knew the rat could chew through a cable or fuel line and bring down the aircraft. Flying a plane with no automatic pilot, he couldn't unbuckle his seat belt and go searching for the beady-eyed varmint. He was confronted with a real danger.

Then he recalled that a rat is a rodent—and without oxygen it would soon die. So he pointed the nose of the plane upward. He climbed a thousand feet, then two, and when he hit the 20,000 foot mark, there was no further noise from the rat—which was found dead when he made the next stop.[2]

Worry is a mental rat that gnaws at your vital beliefs and values (as well as your physical body), and only by rising above the challenge on the wings of faith can you rid yourself of it.

It is my personal belief that more of God's children are challenged with this negative emotion than about any other source of temptation. It can only be countered by the realization that God is sovereign; that He, not circumstances beyond His control, is in charge of your life; and that the promises of His Word are ones He is honor-bound to keep.

No wonder Paul, coming to the end of his warm letter to the Philippians, wrote these words:

> Whatever is true, whatever is noble, whatever is right, whatever is pure, whatever is lovely, whatever is admirable—if anything is excellent or praiseworthy—think about such things. Whatever you have learned or received or heard from me, or seen in me—put it into practice. And the God of peace will be with you (Philippians 4:8-9).

✑

I once heard of a man who was a chronic worrier. If he didn't have legitimate things to worry about, he invented them. If worry had been an Olympic event, surely he would have won the gold.

Finally, a friend said, "I know of a wonderful counselor who can help you." Reluctantly, the man made an appointment.

He had made considerable progress after a few weeks of counseling, and when the two friends met the next time, the chronic worrier seemed happier than he had ever been before.

"It's marvelous what has happened to you!" the friend exclaimed.

"Yes, even though it's costing thousands of dollars, it is certainly worth it."

"But you don't have that kind of money to spend. How will you ever pay the doctor?"

"That's for him to worry about!"

Yes, indeed!

QUESTIONS FOR THOUGHT AND DISCUSSION

Joan's grandmother died of cancer, and her mother also died of that illness. When Joan develops a lump in her breast, she is overwhelmed with worry. She is convinced she has the dreaded disease as well, and that seeing a doctor is futile.

1. In Joan's situation, what would be a healthy concern about this new development? At what point does it become worry and therefore sin? What other response might Joan have to this?

2. Name one thing in your life that causes you to worry. What is the difference between healthy concern about that and sinful worry?

3. What are some ways you can stop the worrying habit?

This Will Hurt...

It will hurt to keep all to yourself something that tempts you to worry. It will hurt to pretend that the worrisome thing is not present. It will hurt to justify your reasons for worrying.

This Will Help…

When something causes you concern, stop and think about what you need to do about it. If there is nothing you can do about it, talk to God about what belongs to Him and what is yours.

Try writing down your worry or worries on a piece of paper. Opposite each item, note who is responsible for the outcome—*you* or *God.* For each one you can do something about, write down what steps you will take to handle the concern. Discipline yourself to get to work on it immediately, even in the face of fear or apathy. For each one that God is responsible for, commit it to Him!

CHAPTER 8

Winning the Battle with Fear

In *Aesop's Fables* there is an old tale that tells of Pestilence meeting a caravan on the road to Baghdad.

"Where are you going in such haste?" the leader of the caravan inquires.

"I am going to Baghdad to take 5000 lives," Pestilence firmly replies. A few days pass, and once more Pestilence and the caravan meet.

"You lied! You lied!" the leader of the caravan shouts. "You took not 5000 lives, but 50,000!"

"No," Pestilence insists, "I took 5000 and not a soul more. It was Fear who killed all the others."

As we learned in the previous chapter, worry is a destructive habit that robs us of peace of mind. Fear, however, goes much deeper than worry. It is potentially one of the most dangerous of all emotions. As a medical doctor told me, "Fears are the most disruptive, destructive things we can have." Fear is also one of the first emotions man encountered after creation. When Adam took the forbidden fruit, he lamented his loss of security: "I was afraid" (Genesis 3:10). He knew he was estranged from God, and that realization brought fear to his heart.

Fear is one of the strongest of all human emotions. I don't need to define it. You know what it is when your heart freezes within and you are paralyzed, wondering what to do. I felt it grip my heart when I got a phone call saying that a close friend and her baby had been kidnapped. The caller stated that she had been drugged and the baby molested. It turned out to be a vicious prank that someone had perpetrated on the friend's family, but all of us felt terrible fear and concern for their safety for the few hours until we learned the truth. To admit the presence of fear isn't weakness. Only a fool would pretend he is never fearful.

General George S. Patton, one of the most courageous generals who ever commanded forces on a battlefield said, "All men are frightened. The more intelligent they are, the more they are frightened. The courageous man is the man who forces himself, in spite of his fear, to carry on."[1]

To admit to having fear is one thing; to be paralyzed by it so you can't do anything about it is another. Later in this chapter I will give you some guidelines that will help you cope. Not all fear is cowardice. It can be your friend, because it causes you to rise to the challenge. It is when you panic and fail to deal effectively with it that you become its victim.

The person who says he is afraid of nothing is either totally ignorant of what's out there or else is a liar! Fear is one of our most formidable enemies, and it comes at us from a variety of sources, often exploiting the hairline cracks in our defenses, rendering us vulnerable, incapacitated, and defeated.

We're All Afraid—Just of Different Things

In response to a series of commentaries I did on this subject on my radio program, here's how some of our *Guidelines* listeners expressed their fears.

- I'm a mother, 26 years old, and I have a terrible fear of death and sickness. I have a daughter 2 years old, and I'm expecting another child. I don't want my children to grow up having the same feelings about life that I have...I just can't get rid of this terrible fear of death and dying.

- My mother died of bilateral breast cancer, and I took care of her and watched her die a terrible death. The fear of contracting this disease hangs over me and is always in the back of my mind.

- I'm very fearful about the future and the present world situation. Is there any real hope that our children may grow up in a normal world?

And there you have three biopsies of the deep fears rooted in the lives of people today. Fears come in all sizes and descriptions. Some fear heights; some fear speaking in front of crowds of people; some fear death; some fear war and destruction; some fear getting sick; some fear growing old; some fear the dark; some being alone; some running out of money before they die; but almost all people when they are honest, regardless of their age or status in life, admit to being afraid of something.

The what-ifs of life. Death is the ultimate robber that takes away your life, but fear is the constant stalker that deprives you of peace of mind and contentment. Be honest and admit it. Do you ever fear the big what-ifs of life—like

- What if I should get sick?
- What if my husband should die?
- What if I should lose my money?
- What if I should be in an accident?
- What if I should get cancer?
- What if my mate should get cancer?
- What if I should be the victim of a terrorist attack?
- What if the plane I am on should crash?

The what-if's of life are absolutely endless. Fear is everybody's problem, right? A poll conducted in the British Isles indicated that almost everybody admits to some kind of fear. One in ten is fearful of the dark. As we grow older, that fear may be of going down a dark alley where danger lurks, or of being alone in an unlighted house.

One person in four is afraid of animals of one kind or another. One person in five is fearful of high places or enclosed places, such as an elevator. Perhaps your hands sweat just thinking about skiing off a cornice with lots of drop beneath you, or jumping out of an airplane with a parachute hoping that it will work, or walking along a mountain trail with a sharp drop to a canyon far below.

> "Of all the liars in the world, sometimes the worst are your own fears."

Four out of every five people suffer from fears over personal inadequacies, such as the fear of failure or other self-related fears that raise their ugly heads. Rudyard Kipling was right when he wrote, "Of all the liars in the world, sometimes the worst are your own fears."

We're born with fears. When you came into the world, you were born with at least two, or possibly three, definite fears. The main one is the fear of falling. Notice how a baby jumps when he or she feels insecure. The second is the fear of loud noises. The third, which perhaps isn't one we are actually born with but develops very quickly, is the fear of abandonment. A child is only a few weeks old when he or she becomes fearful of strangers or unfamiliar, insecure situations.

It doesn't take long for us to develop more fears. Little children often imagine monsters and creatures, which are figments of their imagination; nonetheless, their fears are very real.

As we grow older our fears become a bit more sophisticated. At the onset of puberty, we become conscious of ourselves, and we also become acutely aware that we aren't exactly as graceful as a ballerina or a matador. Teenagers struggle with their self-image, and a lot of their fears focus around personal things—appearance, ability to function and perform, and of course, a very big question mark about the future and the world around them.

Writing for *Decision* magazine, Dr. Millard Sall, a Christian psychologist, observed,

Fear is a universal emotion. Children fear being left alone. Adolescents fear rejection. Young adults fear failure or mediocrity. And older adults fear death or life with no meaning. We fear pain, sickness, desertion and ridicule. We worry about loss of work, loss of a loved one, economic instability and world crisis. Within our hearts we harbor nameless fears that appear only in dreams or as a persistent, unsettling apprehension about life. Fear is common to us all.[2]

The Progression of Fear

A childhood fear of the dark may seem pretty silly to a teenager who, whether or not he admits it, is afraid of rejection by his peer group. That teenage fear isn't much of an issue to his gray-haired grandfather, who fears he may run out of money before he dies. My point is that when we wrestle with fear, it is intensely personal and real to us, the individual who is disturbed by it. It is an inner struggle that a person is going through at a particular time. The depth and intensity of it often cannot be understood by anyone else.

At every point in the journey of life, the things that concern us can create fear. Through my personal experience and through thoughtful observation of human nature, I have noticed that most of our fears fall into two categories: 1) *fear of what we have not personally experienced or do not understand*—something that is not part of our everyday lives that we fear *could* happen; and 2) *fear of what might happen,* regardless of whether or not there is any real basis for expecting it to happen—such as the fear of being struck by a falling star.

The number-one fear of children today, school psychologists report, is that Mommy and Daddy may get divorced. That fear is born of the fact that it has happened to so many of their friends. For nearly 50 percent of all grade-school children in America, that fear has given way to another one: Does Daddy still love me even though he doesn't live with us anymore? The child knows that Daddy rejected Mommy, and he feels rejected as well, especially when Daddy says repeatedly he will do something and then doesn't follow through.

Another strong fear for a youngster is that he might be rejected by his peer group. A child wants to be accepted. He doesn't want to stand out from the crowd. Being different may result in rejection by peers who have become a surrogate family when the child doesn't get acceptance at home.

The fear of failure puts a child under pressure as well. Things like the unrealistic expectation of his parents, the inability to measure up to older brothers and sisters, and not making the team all create fertile ground for the fear of failure.

Often, though it may not be expressed, the love that children receive comes with strings attached. That is how it comes through to the child, at least. A child will perceive these unexpressed expectations: *If you make us proud of you by making good grades, by keeping your room clean, by behaving yourself—then we will love you!* The greater the emphasis on success, the greater the fear of failure a child must cope with.

Many of the fears that children have are "more caught than taught." Their parents and peers have attitudes about or responses to things such as the supernatural, animals, snakes, bats, lizards, death, people of a different race or religion, and a host of other things. The child gets the impression that these are all things to be avoided or feared.

As each of us works through the troubled waters of adolescence and emerges into adulthood, we take with us the same framework that was built during childhood. In addition, the differences between the sexes cause men and women to fear different things.

Women are more prone to fear things that would threaten their relationships: *Are my children doing okay? Can I balance a job and home responsibilities? Does my husband still see me as attractive, or could I lose him to another woman?* Men, on the other hand, are more concerned about their accomplishments: *Could I be passed over for promotion? Do my contemporaries respect me? Am I succeeding in my career?* Men tend to be goal-oriented, whereas women are relationship-oriented. For both men and women, fear keeps us from getting where we want to be.

Senior adults have fears more focused on health issues, which include the fear of death, as well as the fear of running out of money, which is compounded by inflation, an uncertain economy, and increased longevity.

Just as some people are more prone to worry than others are, some do battle with fear on a far more regular basis than do others. If you are one of those stalwart individuals who fears nothing, count yourself fortunate. Nonetheless, you had better not skip this chapter! I've seen people who seemed to fear nothing become absolutely paralyzed in terror when a doctor says, "You have cancer." The big "C" word changed everything for them.

What Should We Fear?

As I mentioned, the entire history of humanity is one that has been painted with dark streaks of fear, beginning with the first family in the Garden of Eden, starting with Adam who explained why he hid from God: "I heard you in the garden, and I was afraid because I was naked; so I hid" (Genesis 3:10).

During World War 2, Franklin Delano Roosevelt encouraged the American people by saying, "The only thing we have to fear is fear itself," a line borrowed from the naturalist Henry David Thoreau who on September 7, 1851, wrote in his journal, "Nothing is so much to be feared as fear."[3] Three centuries before Thoreau, the French essayist Montaigne wrote, "The thing of which I have most to fear is fear."[4]

Is that necessarily true? Should we fear nothing in life but fear itself? I've thought about some of the fears I've had to face at one time or another. Though I haven't struggled with fear as some do, I freely admit to fearing some things.

I'm not afraid of losing my good looks or the wavy black hair I had in my twenties. The latter departed quite a long while ago, and the former was never an issue. I'm not afraid of death or dying, though I'm certainly not in a hurry for it. I am afraid of rattlesnakes. I am afraid of lightning because I was struck by it once as a bolt of lightning came down the shaft of an umbrella and scorched my thumb. But are these fears, or are they rather a healthy appreciation of what could hurt me?

There is something else I include in my category of fear—God! Surprised? I'm not afraid of God the same way I was afraid of a bully who used to pick on me when I was a kid.

"I thought God was a loving Father," you might say. "Don't you believe that?"

"Certainly," I would reply. "I'm convinced of that."

"Then what are you afraid of?"

The great and awesome God who spoke the word and brought our world into existence, the same God who then breathed life into man, isn't on my level. Therefore, I give Him the respect He deserves. Twice Scripture says, "The fear of the LORD is the beginning of wisdom" (Psalm 111:10; Proverbs 9:10). At the same time, the New Testament says that perfect love drives out fear (see 1 John 4:18). I know that God loves me, and I have learned to love Him in return. The relationship we have is one of a father and son. I'm not afraid of God in the way I would be if that relationship did not exist.

But I do reverence Him. Theologians refer to this as a "reverential trust." I understand how great and mighty our heavenly Father is, but I have no fear of His wrath because I know, as a child of God, I will never be a target of it.

Understanding the Concern of God

The greater my understanding of the nature of God and His care and concern for my life, the less will be my fear of many of the issues that paralyze people today. There is a marked relationship between your fears and what you know about God—either correctly or incorrectly. If your concept of God is distorted, possibly because of the image of God you had growing up, what you fear may be irrational. A true understanding of God changes all of that. As I wrote in my book *Today Can Be Different,*

> What comes to mind as you think about God reveals a great deal about your life; and on the basis of what you tell me about God, I can in all probability tell you a good deal about your fears. Your concept of God is to your life what a foundation is to a house, what a periodic chart is to research in a laboratory. It is a fundamental in setting parameters of reality and behavior.[5]

Many people know a great deal about God without really knowing Him. They may commute from the world to the church for an hour a week to enjoy the music and a motivational talk about being a success in life (we used to call this a sermon). They lack a deeper understanding of God, which includes theology, and so they have a smattering of ideas, much like a handful of fine pearls without any string to hold them together to form a necklace. Subsequently, fear is one of the issues they wrestle with, because they are uncertain as to whether God really is personal, powerful, and a "stronghold in the day of trouble," as the prophet Nahum wrote some six centuries before Christ.

Not All Fear Is Bad

Adam knew fear because he had broken his fellowship with God. The consequences of that took him outside of God's will for his life. At times fear is a marvelous thing. It creates a healthy appreciation of consequences for wrongdoing, and it serves as a motivation to safeguard our health, or our family, or whatever we consider meaningful.

I have a healthy appreciation of cancer—but I'm not afraid of it. I've already had my first slight bout with it, and that was enough to now send me to the doctor on a regular basis.

A friend of mine, however, refuses to see a doctor on a regular basis. This type of fear can be deadly. Her mother died of cancer by the time she was 50 years old, and my friend is too fearful that she may eventually succumb to the same thing.

In the New Testament, two different words are used, both of which are translated as *fear*. The first group of words relates to the Greek word root *phob-*. We get our word *phobia* from it. The word generally means "to be afraid" or "to become frightened." It is also used in regard to people, where it means "to show respect" or "to have reverence."[6]

The second word and its derivatives relate to the Greek word *deiliao*, which means "to be timid" or "to be cowardly."[7] It is significant that this is the word Paul used when he said, "God has not given us a spirit of fear and timidity, but of power, love, and self-discipline" (2 Timothy 1:7 NLT). This kind of fear—or timidity—is the kind that keeps you from seeing your doctor when you have chest pains. This kind of fear causes people to become its prisoner, which is contrary to all that God has for you.

How Do You Cope with Fear?

Ridicule is not the way to cope with fear! Telling a child that it is silly to be afraid of the dark only frustrates him. When a parent makes light of his fear, the child will also feel shame.

An elderly parent, who sees that the stock market is eroding and is afraid he may not have enough money to carry him through old age, cannot simply be told, "Dad, you've got lots of money—there's no need to fear!" That doesn't bring the same relief that can be his by your taking the time to go over his finances, analyze his insurance policies and health care, and project a variety of scenarios to show him that there *is* enough money. And, if there is not enough money, work out a solution he is comfortable with to allay his concern and fear. When an elderly person is afraid of what's going to happen to him, you can say, "You have nothing to fear!" Or you can take your Bible and remind him that God promises to meet all of our needs. The second option brings more comfort.

When someone is afraid, ridicule, criticism, or minimizing the fear doesn't work. Logic doesn't always work either, because fear is an emotional response; it is not based on reason.

The following are some guidelines that will help you cope with fear when it looms on your horizon and threatens to assault you.

Guideline 1: Admit your fear. This means getting it out in the open. Talk about it. Face it head-on. Stare it down. Fears that are ignored tend to grow greater, but fears confronted tend to shrink in size and intensity. As Craig Massey wrote,

> One deeply rooted fear invariably spawns countless other fears and each gains strength from the other until the whole world seems to close in on our unwilling victim.[8]

Sometimes, we expect God to do things for us that He wants us to do for ourselves. Confronting your fear is something you must do before you seek and find God's help with what you cannot do for yourself.

We are often like the little child who would repeatedly take the kitchen broom outside to play with it; then he would leave it behind when his mother called him for dinner. One evening, his father looked for the broom and could not find it. "Son," he asked, "were you playing with the broom before dinner?"

"Yes, Daddy."

"Then go outside and get the broom," he said.

"But Daddy, it's dark outside, and I'm afraid."

"Nothing to be frightened of, son," his father replied. "God's out there, so go out and get the broom."

Reluctantly, the little boy opened the door. "God, if you are out there, would you please get me the broom!"

God is out there in the dark, but He still expects you to get the broom! You yourself have to confront the fear that is in the dark.

In my book *Coffee Cup Counseling*, I describe the following scenario:

> Your friend Joy misses Bible study for several weeks, and you drop by to see her. As you sit down for a cup of tea together, you let her know that she has been missed. At first she talks about the baby sitter who couldn't take care of the children, but then she bursts into tears and says, "Oh, I might as well tell you what's really bothering me. I don't know what's gotten into me, but lately whenever I start to back out the car, my hands get cold and sweaty and my heart beats like crazy. I'm scared to death that I'm going to get hit by another car. I don't know what's the matter with me. Dean says I must be losing my mind. Do you think I'm crazy?"[9]

To say to Joy, "It's dumb to be afraid to drive. You've just got to do it," only creates greater apprehension. At times, telling someone what bothers us and what we are afraid of is in itself therapy.

It is my belief that every person needs someone in whom he can confide to serve as a sounding board, who will keep his confidence, who will give him the freedom to say whatever is on his mind without ridicule, without being judgmental or rejecting him. This is what professionals do, yet the responsibility to help others in this way rests on all of us who are part of the family of God.

Discovering a tiny lump in your breast can strike fear in your heart. Immediately, your hands get cold and clammy and you think, *That's cancer!* I have known some individuals who absolutely became paralyzed with fear upon finding something or experiencing something that could possibly be a threat to their health or welfare.

A doctor friend of mine says that people are always coming to him with imagined symptoms of cancer. Yet when he begins to talk with them and explore their family medical background, he discovers that no one in their family has ever had cancer, and a physical exam or a mammogram doesn't reveal any indication whatsoever of a problem. This is not to suggest that routine physicals are not important. They are! But living with a constant fear of what has not happened but that you fear might happen robs you of peace of mind and contentment. Fear is an emotion that needs to be confronted. It can work for you or deprive you of your happiness.

Doing nothing is the worst possible scenario! The longer you neglect a potential problem and refuse to confront your fear, the more devastating the situation can become.

Find out! Call your doctor and make an appointment, and the sooner the better. It is what you don't know that can kill you. Discovering that something is not life-threatening allays your fear and brings peace of mind. Living with the "what-if" or "if only" puts you in the cave of fear. It's not worth it.

Guideline 2: Assess the strength of what you fear. Confronting your fear is always the first step toward a solution, but confronting it doesn't always eliminate it. The next step is to get the spotlight on it and see how large or small it really is. Then for a moment ask yourself, *What is the worst-case scenario?* Then ask yourself, *Is God greater than my fear?* David had the conviction that God was. He was a shepherd boy who took his father's flocks from Bethlehem toward the Dead Sea to greener pastures during the winter months. To get there he had to traverse a valley that was known as "The Valley of the Shadow of Death"—a literal place near the Inn of the Good Shepherd on the road that today leads from Jerusalem to Jericho.

Even after 3000 years the geography there hasn't changed. Steep sides of the valley run top to bottom, and the shepherd would of necessity have to take his flock through that valley—no problem when the weather was good, but when cloudbursts (which occasionally happen in this seismic fault known as the Jordan Valley) came, the shepherd and his flock could be caught by the raging waters. That fact makes David's words, "Yea, though I walk through the valley of the shadow of death, I will fear no evil for you are with me," more meaningful.

> Is it necessary to eliminate or directly deal with everything you fear? As surprising as it may seem, my answer is, "No!"

Yes, he knew what he faced, but he also knew the Shepherd of his soul was with him—something you can know as well.

Dr. Karl Menninger believed that you can draw a continuum between the ability to cope with life and the inability to cope with it—between sanity and insanity, if you will. But on this continuum, there is no clearly defined place at which you have moved from one side to the other. Every person goes through periods in life when he or she is better able to do battle with his or her inner struggles, and that includes fear.

So, is it necessary to eliminate or directly deal with everything you fear? As surprising as it may seem, my answer is, "No!" Some things just don't matter. You can sidestep them, tunnel around them, or flat-out avoid them. Let me illustrate.

I thought I knew my wife pretty well before we married. For three years we had dated, and I expected no surprises when we said, "I do!" Six months into our marriage found us in Paris, and in between conferences we were doing some of the usual tourist things. To see the Eiffel Tower was on the "must do" list, and to save money, we decided to take the elevator up the Eiffel Tower and walk down. Fine! What we didn't know at the time is that the staircase is exterior, which means it winds back and forth down the outside of the tower. (At its completion in 1889, the Eiffel Tower was the world's tallest structure—some 300 meters or 975 feet in height, the equivalent of a 97-story building.)

We had gone down only a few flights of stairs when I learned something new about my wife: Darlene suffers from fear of heights—*acrophobia*. She does fine when she is close to the ground, but get her close to the edge of anything with a sheer drop and she freezes. The same thing happened again when we tried skiing. When she froze, I said, "It's okay, honey. You don't have to ski downhill." We switched to cross-country skiing and everybody is happy. Not all fears have to be overcome. Forget skydiving or walking on trails at the edge of sheer drops!

Guideline 3: Act upon your fear. In his best-selling book *Rome 1960: The Olympics That Changed the World,* David Maraniss tells how Ingrid Kraemer faced her fear and triumphed over it, eventually winning the coveted gold medal in the 3-meter springboard diving competition. You see, as a child Ingrid had a phobia about hurting herself when she didn't dive precisely and failed to enter the water properly. "I had real problems of fear in my first years," she admitted, adding, "I wasn't courageous at all. I had to work hard on it and only bit by bit managed to overcome it."[10]

Her father, realizing that Ingrid had talent but no future in competitive diving unless she conquered her fear, made a special vest of rubber foam so she would not hurt herself when she hit the water on her back or stomach.

Most fears need to be confronted, such as fear about your health or whether you will be injured by diving into a pool or entering an elevator; and some fears can be accommodated. Some people have jobs that require travel, yet they are afraid of flying on airplanes. What about the woman who has a job as a sales representative but is afraid to fly? Should she grit her teeth and tough it out?

I have been on flights sitting next to individuals who were stricken with fear. I'm thinking of the time I turned to the young woman sitting next to me and casually remarked, "Flying gives you a hard time, right?" "Yes," she said, "but how could you tell?" "That's my jacket you keep rolling up in a wad," I commented with a smile.

Some think that the only way to beat the fear of flying is to drown it, and those seated beside them usually learn about the person's fear after his second drink. At times, counseling helps eliminate the problem by getting the fear out in the open and talking about it. Even with the fear of flying, therapy groups have successfully helped people overcome that fear by giving them exposure to the mechanics of planes and flying.

Some people have had inordinate fears about computers or telephone recorders, and they have, through experience, come to learn that these are simply mechanical devices that do what they are told to do. A computer will not reach out and bite the hand that feeds it a DVD or CD, and an answering machine cannot read your mind.

The fear of death has been called man's greatest fear. Who would deny that any unexpected encounter with death creates fear? Most of us can appreciate Mark Twain's comment that he wished he knew where he was going to die, because if he did, he would never go near the place.

When a doctor says, "If you know how to pray, you had better do so, because medical science has nothing to offer," you may be gripped with cold fear. In reality, every person on Planet Earth is terminal.

When a wealthy Easterner contracted tuberculosis, his doctor advised him to go Out West where the air was dry and less polluted. One warm afternoon, the man drove off the freeway into a small Arizona cow town and stopped his car in front of the local post office. In front were several cowpokes, who eyed the stranger as he hit the button to roll down the car window. Making eye contact with one of the men, he said, "You over there—could you tell me what the death rate in this town is?"

Pausing for a moment, the cowboy replied, "Same as it is back where you came from, Mister—just one to a person!"

The genealogies in the book of Genesis show this ongoing litany: A father begot a son and died; then the son became a father, who had a son, and he died. We need to remember that matters of life and death are in God's hands. Acting upon your fear means that you do what you can and find God's help to go beyond your strength.

J.C. Penney cut man's greatest fear down to size. At the height of the Great Depression, Penney was losing everything he had worked so hard for. He ended up in the hospital with ulcers that threatened his life. His diet was milk and crackers. His nerves were on edge. And he was very much afraid that he was dying.

While he lay in bed, he heard the words of a song drift down the corridors of the hospital, "Be not dismayed whate'er betide; God will take care of you…" Those words sank into his heart, and according to Penney's own testimony, they turned his life around. His fear vanished and his faith in God's care grew.

The Bible declares that life and death are not matters of indifference to our heavenly Father. He has numbered the very hairs of our head and knows when the sparrow falls to the ground. This, of course, must be taken by faith, and faith is what puts fear to flight.

Believing that God is a good God and that He cares about you is a powerful antidote to the venom of fear. This was the confident assurance expressed so often by the psalmist, King David.

Dr. Jack Morris, a pastor and psychotherapist, often asks his patients who are struggling with fear to memorize David's Psalm 23—a great antidote to fear—and recite it aloud several times a day. In Psalm 118:6-7, David says, "The LORD is with me; I will not be afraid. What can man do to me? The LORD is with me; he is my helper."

With such confidence, it is no wonder that David cried out, "The LORD is my light and my salvation—whom shall I fear? The LORD is the stronghold of my life—of whom shall I be afraid?" (Psalm 27:1). The assurance that God is with you, that His actual presence surrounds you, that nothing can happen to you apart from His will, cuts life's greatest fears down to size.

Acting upon your fear means acknowledging whatever it is that threatens to keep you from where you want to go or doing what you want to do—and then developing an action plan and moving ahead. There are two ways you can do this. You can have a daring and audacious disregard for reality, or you can have a greater inner strength—one that comes from the assurance that you are not alone, that the Shepherd of your soul walks with you—and confidently move forward. As actress Dorothy Bernard put it, "Courage is fear that has said its prayers."

Confronting his fear and moving ahead was a tough decision for Robert Nichols after probably the most frightening experience of his life, going far beyond anything he had ever experienced as a paramedic working with all kinds of crises.

You see, Robert, along with my son Steve and another climbing buddy, were scaling the face of El Capitan (the largest single piece of granite in the world), located in California's Yosemite National Park. Robert was leading the climb, when the gear holding him securely to the face of the rock became disengaged, and he plunged downward some 40 feet, or the equivalent of four floors of a building. The valley floor was more than 2800 feet below them.

When Robert fell, the first piton pulled loose, but then—thank God— the next one anchoring my son held. Had the piton holding Steve securely been jerked loose, the weight of the two men would quite probably have pulled the third loose and all three would have lost their lives.

Robert described what happened: "You feel your body traveling faster and faster, time stretches longer and longer in a real Einsteinian way." No lasting damage was done, however, and they recovered their position. Then Steve and Robert talked and prayed together. "If you don't take the lead pitch and climb right away," Steve told him, "you will never climb again." After a few minutes, Robert courageously started climbing again, one handhold and then another, one foothold and then another.

When you are hanging on to the face of a solid piece of granite and it has taken you five days of torturous climbing to get to where you are, you don't just hike back to the car and go home. "There is *no* alternative but to go on," wrote Robert describing what happened, adding, "I felt drained, but repeating 'God is my strength and my shield' managed to displace the fear and filled me with hope that we would safely reach our goal."

Was Robert fearful? Of course. Who wouldn't be? But he didn't quit. Speaking of the incident later, Steve said, "Fear is not something you overcome; it's something you manage."

Hebrews tells of those who don't manage the fear of death, those "who all their lives were held in slavery by their fear of death" (Hebrews 2:15). And is there hope for them? Or are they doomed to live with a gun under their pillow, with their prescriptions lining the counter, and their blinds drawn so no one will know if they are home? There is hope available by putting into practice the next guideline.

Guideline 4: Commit to the Lord what you cannot change or understand. As long as you are alive, there will be situations that will strike fear into your heart. "When we came into Macedonia," Paul wrote to the

Corinthians, "this body of ours had no rest, but we were harassed at every turn—conflicts on the outside, fears within. But God, who comforts the downcast, comforted us" (2 Corinthians 7:5-6).

"Aren't you afraid to travel internationally?" some people ask me, and I respond, "No, because I do believe that safety is not the absence of danger but rather it is the presence of the Lord." Before I go anywhere, I first pray, and then when I am relatively sure He wants me to go, I strive to put myself in His hands and refuse to be afraid. I'm convinced there are some fears God never intended us to bear, and when we try to handle our load and His, we're not going to make it.

An elderly Christian lady, after having read that God neither slumbers nor sleeps, shut off her light with the comment, "Why should both of us stay awake tonight?" Good reasoning. Someone with a flair for details counted 365 "fear nots" in the Bible, one for every day of the year.

For the Christian, the fear issue is framed in a different dimension than is the case with the nonbeliever. That dimension is the God element. Is there a God who is in control of my life, let alone the universe, or do the promises of Scripture mean absolutely nothing? *Like what?* you may be thinking. Like the precious verses found in Isaiah 43, where God says when you go through the deep waters and face the rivers that could drown you, He will be with you. Neither, He promised, will the fire burn you.

Those promises were not made to spiritual giants as Elijah, or David, or Billy Graham, or the pastor of your church. Those promises have your name attached to them, provided you will accept them and believe them.

Guideline 5: Rest in the promises of God's Word. It is here that a knowledge of Scripture and what it says becomes an antidote to debilitating fear. Have you really discovered what the Bible says about fear and overcoming it? Take a concordance and look up the word *fear*. You will read encouraging words such as these:

- "Surely God is my salvation; I will trust and not be afraid" (Isaiah 12:2).

- "Do not fear, for I am with you; do not be dismayed, for I am your God. I will strengthen you and help you; I will uphold you with my righteous right hand" (Isaiah 41:10).

- "Yea, though I walk through the valley of the shadow of death, I will fear no evil; for You are with me" (Psalm 23:4 NKJV).

- "When I am afraid, I will trust in you" (Psalm 56:3).

- "Have no fear of sudden disaster or of the ruin that overtakes the wicked" (Proverbs 3:25).

- "Fear not, little flock; for it is your Father's good pleasure to give you the kingdom" (Luke 12:32 KJV).

You will also hear the words of Jesus:

> "Never will I leave you; never will I forsake you." So we say with confidence, "The Lord is my helper; I will not be afraid. What can man do to me?" (Hebrews 13:5-6).

Perhaps the most important thing you will learn is that you don't have to be afraid when you know God is with you. In times of stress you can "lean upon the Word," resting in the promises of the Book.

Guideline 6: Remember the source of your fear. God? Usually not. Satan, as the enemy of your soul, makes you want to doubt God's power, makes you feel that you are alone and that God is distant, weak, or distracted. He makes you want to think you are strictly on your own when the lights go out or when you are confronted with a challenge to your health and well-being. Paul was explicit when he said that this debilitating kind of fear does not come from heaven. Memorize these words: *"God has not given us a spirit of fear"* (2 Timothy 1:7 NKJV). Write them on your soul.

Back in the days when circuses went from town to town, a prominent circus featured an act with Bengal tigers, those beautiful beasts that look like overgrown housecats but whose powerful claws are capable of shredding an enemy in a few swipes. As part of the tiger routine, a trainer would go into the cage with his whip and a small kitchen chair. The snap of his whip would prod the tigers into a routine which was perfunctory yet dangerous. Bengal tigers are ferocious, and natives who live where they roam in the wilds are always frightened of them. And with good cause.

On one occasion the trainer went into the cage, and with the door locked behind him, started his routine. Then, without warning, the lights went out. For approximately 30 seconds, says Thomas Butts in *Tigers in the Dark,* the trainer was locked in with the tigers.

When the lights came on, he finished his performance almost as though nothing unusual or unexpected had happened. Afterwards he was asked how he felt when he knew that in the dark the tigers could see him, but he couldn't see them. They knew where he was, but he didn't know where they were. He admitted that at first he was gripped with a chilling fear. Then he remembered that while he knew the tigers could see him, they didn't know that he *couldn't* see them. Score evened! And he continued snapping his whip and talking to them just as he would have had the lights been on.[11]

What an experience! There are times—perhaps not as dramatic but equally important—when the lights go out on you and you are left in the dark. It happens when the doctor mentions the big "C" word—you have cancer! Or you face an unexpected layoff, or a tragedy confronts you. The light of your life is dimmed, if not snuffed out.

That's when you have no choice but to rely on what you know—not what you see. Like what? You know that God hasn't singled you out as a target of His wrath, that storms confront everyone. You know God will honor the promises of His Word. You also know that while the lights may have gone out on you, they haven't gone out on God. He sees the whole situation very clearly even though you don't. If you are His child, you also know that nothing that happens to you is beyond the sovereign care of your heavenly Father.

Guideline 7: Remember, nothing is forever. The darkness passes. The illness subsides. What you feared didn't take place—or if it did, God was there to walk with you during the dark night of your soul. The following well illustrates the path to take when you are gripped with fear.

On May 19, 1780, "an unusual darkening of the day sky was observed over the New England states and parts of Canada,"[12] blotting out the sun. In Connecticut, the darkness forced the Governor's Council to light candles to see. Fearing that the darkness was the judgment of God, one senator made a motion to adjourn. But wise old Abraham Davenport rose to his feet and counseled otherwise.

"It is either the Day of Judgment," he began, "or it is not. If it is not, there is no need of adjourning. If it is, I desire to be found doing my duty. I move that candles be brought and that we proceed to business."

An unknown poet put it,

> Bring in the candles! Keep to the task!
> What more can judgment angels ask?
> Bring in the candles! Let us be found
> Doing our duty's daily round.

That's what the tiger trainer did when the lights went out. He fearlessly kept on snapping his whip, talking to the animals as though nothing had happened. And that's what they did in New England the day the sun was darkened and refused to shine.

So when the lights go out on you, carry on, never running, never yielding to fear, doing what you know God wants you to do—and then in His time, the lights will come on again.

QUESTIONS FOR THOUGHT AND DISCUSSION

❦

Robert and Steven were rock climbing when one of the pitons pulled out. Robert plummeted through the air almost 40 feet before Steven was able to stop his fall. For a time, Robert was frozen in panic, and Steven helped him overcome the fear so Robert had the confidence to continue with the climb.

1. What are some of the thoughts that might be going through Robert's mind that keep him frozen in fear? If you were Steve, how would you help Robert keep climbing?

2. What is one concern in your personal life that has turned into fear? Try to set aside the paralyzing feelings for a moment to think about the circumstances objectively. Do they warrant that amount of fear? What are some things that set you up for letting a legitimate concern turn into fear that freezes you in action? These might be past experiences, or watching someone else go through something similar, and so on.

3. Describe, in your own words, God's tender care for you in the past. How might focusing on God's help in the past encourage you to put this present fear in perspective?

4. What is one fear in your life that you have avoided facing? Why do you hesitate to confront this fear? What have you read in this chapter that has given you encouragement to begin dealing with this? What are the small, incremental steps you can take?

This Will Hurt...

Sometimes, when someone else has a fear that is not real for you, you might be tempted to dismiss it as silly or not important. It does no good to tell the person that there is nothing to worry about, or to remind him of the good things in life. Fear, whatever the source, is very real to the person who is feeling it. It will hurt to remind the person that there is "nothing to fear but fear itself."

This Will Help...

Some fears are never eliminated entirely, but they can be managed so you do not live frozen by their influence. It will help to reassure the person that fear is normal, and that we all have different fears. Be a sounding board for someone who is afraid, and suspend judgment about their feelings. The age-old advice of putting yourself in another person's shoes is good. Imagine yourself with his background and his situation and try to understand his fears instead of dismissing them.

Chapter 9

Boredom—When
Your Emotions Flatline

Hearing the staccato bleep of a heart monitor when the pattern first gets erratic and then flatlines is a frightening experience, especially when it is connected to someone you love. When that happens, alarms sound and medical personnel rush to assist the person who lies in a hospital bed. There is a window of no more than ten minutes during which the patient can be revived. Scary? Absolutely! Yet when your emotions begin to flatline—the result of too many things thrown at you—rarely does anyone take notice. They simply close down and leave you exhausted, bored, and numb. Yes, you are still alive, but life has lost its zip, and you get up and mechanically plod through another day. You can relate to the sign that reads, "Tomorrow cancelled for lack of interest!"

In her book *The Feminine Mystique,* Betty Friedan included a chapter entitled "The Problem That Has No Name." She discussed the plight of many women around the world. Such was the feeling of a 20-year-old mother, who put it in these words:

I ask myself why I am so dissatisfied. I've got my health, fine children, a lovely new home, enough money. My husband has a real future as an electronics engineer. He doesn't have any of these feelings. He says, maybe I need a vacation, but that isn't it! I can't sit down and read a book alone. If the children are napping, I just walk through the house waiting for them to wake up. Then you wake up one morning, and there's nothing to look forward to![1]

The problem Betty Friedan says has no name is often described as boredom. It's the result of what happens when your emotions flatline. It's a problem shared by people from all classes and ranks of people. What you have or what you don't have is no guarantee that you can't fall prey to this insidious thing and become its victim. Rich and poor, gifted and neglected, intellectuals and those who are somewhat dull are all found in the ranks of the bored. Said Harry Johnson, a medical doctor,

> Today's civilization, the most advanced in history, with the highest standard of living ever known, has produced a generation of bored, apathetic people. We seek entertainment, yet find it dull—even a great performance in the theater is often rewarded by hordes of people leaving before the curtain falls. We sit in front of TV sets watching a succession of plays, shows, and movies without really noticing what we are seeing. We leaf aimlessly through newspapers and magazines. When we say, "I'm tired," many of us really mean, "I'm tired of what I'm doing. I'm tired of my way of life."[2]

Living in a World That's Bored

If you question the fact that ours is a tired and often bored generation, ponder the words of Steven Winn, who is the Arts and Culture Critic for the *San Francisco Chronicle*:

> Type the word into Google and scores of Web sites devoted to boredom abatement are on offer. Spend any time with a

teenager and this ripe, Olympian judgment—on a TV show, a friend, a plan for the evening, life itself—is sure to resound: "Bor-ing!" Critics, with only a touch more tact, can kiss off a new play or symphony with the quietly damning assertion that they were bored.[3]

Notice that most news programs not only have a reporter talking, but also a breaking news tape at the bottom, often with factoids imbedded on the screen as well. Cell-phone makers such as Motorola routinely include games such as Snake, solitaire, and Tetris to prevent boredom. Social networks like YouTube and Facebook are designed to turn those dull in-between moments into something exciting.

> Boredom...is one of the reasons that both men and women walk out the door and never come back.

A businessman went to his doctor complaining of feeling bad, though he couldn't pinpoint the trouble. The doctor ordered laboratory tests and gave the man a thorough examination, but they didn't turn up any real physical problem. The man came back for further consultation. After a few words of pleasantries, the doctor turned to him and said, "I have good news for you. The physical exam hasn't turned up a single problem whatsoever. I can give you a clean bill of health."

Instead of being elated, the man complained, "Doctor, I am tired from the minute I get up in the morning until I go to bed at night." The doctor wisely recognized the man's problem as not physical in nature. He saw that the problem was boredom and began pointing out all the advantages in life that had come to this man—a good business, a nice home, almost everything money could buy, as well as an attractive wife, and children. Bluntly, the man responded, "They can have it—I'm bored stiff with it."

Boredom is not only one of the major causes of fatigue—that listless feeling that leaves you constantly tired out—but it is also one of the factors contributing to broken homes. It is one of the reasons that both men and women walk out the door and never come back.

The Relationship of Boredom to Fatigue

For a moment, think with me about your own life—the day that you had last week when nothing seemed to go right, the day you were constantly interrupted. Perhaps it wasn't last week; maybe it was yesterday. Or maybe it was a whole week of days that seem to blur together.

Every time you started to get to your work, something happened. The phone rang. Somebody dropped by for a friendly chat. You would have liked to say, "Friend, I'd like to sit and talk for a while, but I don't have the time." But you were afraid of offending him, so you sat and killed more time. Each time you got started with your work, you were interrupted again, and again, and again. All the time, you had the burden of your work hanging over your head. At the end of the day, you reviewed your accomplishments, which were zero-minus. You really didn't do anything but answer a few e-mails, but you went home tired out...from the work? No! From the tension that produced the weariness.

Then, the next day, you were able to work your game plan. You got started promptly and things came together. You were able to connect with your customers. Interruptions were at a minimum. That night when you went home, you felt great. Actually, you expended more energy than you did when you were so frustrated, but the difference is that accomplishment defeated fatigue. When people begin to lose interest in their lives, feeling that it is a rat race or a squirrel-cage existence—the same thing day after day after day—they begin to suffer from weariness. Weariness is a gnawing tiredness that can't be defeated by vitamins or pills.

When Dr. Edward Thorndike of Columbia University conducted a series of experiments relating boredom to fatigue, he kept a group of students awake for almost a week by constantly changing their interests. Dr. Thorndike concluded his tests with the following statement: "Boredom is the only real cause of fatigue." (Don't think for a moment that if you are sufficiently interested in what you do, you can give up getting a good night's sleep on a regular basis!) If you recognize that part of your weariness is really caused by boredom, you can follow the prescription for its cure and get a new grip on life.

When Your Emotions Flatline in Marriage

When you flatline emotionally, not only does weariness take its toll on your body physically, but it takes its toll on your marriage in general and in your intimacy in particular. When a couple begins to take each other for granted, their relationship loses excitement. It's dull and mechanical—perfunctory. When she says, "I'm too tired tonight," she really is telling the truth. But when either a husband or a wife gets the "too tired" excuse repeatedly, the other feels rejection. It's like coming to the dinner table night after night only to find that there is nothing on your plate. You feel you deserve better than you are getting.

Both men and women have told me, "I've been to the doctor and he says that there is nothing wrong with me physically. It's just that we're no longer attracted to each other." And when that happens, temptations that would previously have been ignored become more difficult to pass up. Though the individual knows it is wrong, a person who feels rejected finds himself or herself enjoying the attention of someone who seems to have the personality and excitement that first attracted the person to his or her mate.

In most cases, however, the problem is not physical—it's emotional. Psychiatrist Dr. A. Dixon Weatherhead used to say, "Some say it is all in our head; and they are almost right, for most of it is."[4] A study done at Mayo Clinic of 235 patients who complained of physical weariness—the kind that they could not shake—revealed that only 15 percent had anything wrong physically. Even then, in most cases it was not a serious affliction.[5]

The dangerous phases. Statistically, there are three dangerous periods in marriage. The first period, as you might expect, is during the first couple of years, when a couple really begins to know each other. The problems during this period are those of adjustment, not boredom. There's generally plenty of passion. The second critical period is after a couple has been married for seven to ten years, when they have settled down into a routine. By then they usually have two cars, children, and a mortgage on a house, and they are beginning to think, *Is this all there is to life?* The third period of stress comes when a couple has been married for twenty to twenty-five years. The children are grown, and the couple is fortysomething and facing the physical and emotional changes of middle age.

By this time, he is struggling with "the 3 B's": bulges, balding, and bifocals. She no longer looks good in a two-piece swimsuit at the beach. She's seriously interested in Botox for damage repair. Both have aged, and both sometimes wonder if they still have what it takes to attract members of the opposite sex. "My wife isn't the woman I married," complained a very middle-aged man who was attracted to his secretary, a woman a decade younger who didn't show the wear and tear of raising kids. "Yes," I said, "and neither are you the man she married."

Though men are more prone to want to prove to themselves that they still are able to charm someone else, both men and women can become bored with their mates—wrong as that is. There is no more reason for a husband and a wife to allow themselves to grow bored with each other than there is to grow bored with putting money in the bank.

In marriage, the deadly virus of boredom can infect us in many ways. It infects us when we allow ourselves to take each other for granted, when we begin to presume upon each other, and when we lose the freshness and sparkle of romance in a relationship. The process of courtship or dating serves as a time when a couple can really get to know each other. But it also serves to meet an important need that we have all our lives for something called "companionship"—a need that doesn't go away with receding hairlines and wrinkles.

The quiet evenings when you once strolled through the park or by the beach in the moonlight served to meet emotional needs for both of you. But in some cases when a man crosses the threshold of marriage, he allows himself to think, *I've conquered her heart—I've got her. She is my wife now.* He no longer sees any need to take his wife out, open her car door, or spend an evening together in a little restaurant that used to be their favorite haunt. "Why bother to buy flowers?" said a friend, adding, "They just die!"

Losing touch. Our emotions—love, passion, excitement, joy—begin to go flat in marriage when a couple begins to lose touch with each other. That can happen in a variety of ways, especially when financial pressure forces couples to live in different worlds with different friends and colleagues. Men end up spending far more time with women who work in the same office or company than with their wives, and vice versa.

Communication is a mutual exchange of ideas, thoughts, attitudes, information, and feelings between two people. Sometimes when a couple has been married for a dozen years or so, they stop talking. One communications expert says that there are more than 400,000 ways you can communicate nonverbally, but that doesn't cut it when it comes to expressing your emotions and feelings. Some think they have said everything there is to say. Others encounter difficulties expressing themselves ("It doesn't do any good trying to get through to that man!") and bury their thoughts and feelings in television or hide behind women's magazines. Yes, women talk to other women, men talk to other men, but the couple whose marriage is stressed grow further apart and more bored with each other. The problem is not that people grow tired of marriage; they grow tired of each other because they haven't kept their relationship alive.

Your Relationship with God Begins to Flatline

There is another aspect to the problem of boredom, and that has to do with the intertwining of the spiritual with every phase of your life. Boredom comes to us when we begin to lose touch with God, and this often happens at the same time we begin to lose touch with a spouse. You can't compartmentalize your life, calling one area physical, another emotional, and a third spiritual. When the level of excitement begins to drop in life and you begin to grow weary of the routine, your emotional level sinks in all three areas. That is why we often see spiritual backsliding at the same time as general boredom.

Let's go back to something very fundamental, a reminder of what we discussed in chapter 3. You came from the drawing board of heaven as an emotional individual. God made you in such a way that it was His design for you to express your emotions—not stifle, sedate, or suppress them. Reviving the emotional side of your nature is something that needs to be done, something only you can do. So what are some things that can help you with this?

Guideline 1: Start with your very personal self. What you do may depend upon your marital status as well as your sex. Your first challenge, however, is to break out of the box you've put your emotions in and redis-cover that it's okay to feel, to emote, to express yourself. Start by getting physical exertion—preferably outdoors. Do something physical—hike, climb, jog, bike, ski, dig up your garden—whatever it takes to make you break out in a sweat. Of course, you don't want to do this! You'd rather park yourself in front of the TV, your lap laden with junk food that sedates your ennui. You would rather read a romantic novel, or perhaps an exciting one that will transport you into a make-believe world.

It helps some people at the end of each day to journal, keeping track of what emotions they felt that day and how they expressed them.

Interacting with people is important. If you're single, get involved in a singles group. What about Internet groups such as E-Harmony or something similar to that? While it may work for some people, I don't get too excited about this kind of interaction, based on the number of individuals I know personally who have been disappointed or emotion-ally burned by this kind of long-distance relationship. Church-related functions where there is person-to-person contact are the best.

Guideline 2: Rediscover passion in your marriage. Your emotions are very much like a small stream that meanders through a lush green valley with lavender, red, and yellow flowers sprinkled like stardust on the verdant landscape. Then visualize someone damming up the stream, putting boulders and branches across it so the water slowly backs up into a small pond. You, seeing what has happened, take your foot or a stick and punch a hole in the dam, letting the waters flow freely. The point is this: You see the problem and create a new channel for the water, which then makes its way toward the end of the valley.

When your emotions flatline, there's a reservoir inside that begins to build and seeks expression one way or another. If your marriage is boring, don't place the entire blame on your spouse. Realize that you contributed to the staleness that has taken the excitement you once had and anesthetized your feelings. In chess, a "stalemate" means that you can't legally move your player; but in marriage a "stale mate" means you have lost the excitement you once had and your marriage is in big trouble. When men feel sexual rejection, they also feel justified in seeking their sexual thrills in ways that undermine and can destroy what has been a good marriage through either illicit sexual relations such as Internet sex or prostitution, or more likely vicarious thrills such as pornography. But this is not exclusively a male problem. Women are sexual beings and may likewise strive to find excitement in the wrong places as well.

So what's wrong with pornography, especially if your spouse doesn't know about it? I submit the following:

1. *Pornography is fantasy—not reality.* The models who bare their bodies usually don't have stretch marks from giving birth to children. And the blemishes have been covered by cosmetics and skillful editing. In other words, they aren't reality; nor is what the filmmaker portrays "real life." Instead of loving each other, those who indulge in porn fantasize, making love with the slick centerfold or the girl in the flick. What really turns a man on is not how sexy your body is but that you want him as badly as he wants you.

2. *Pornography is demeaning to women.* It cheapens them. Without saying a word, a wife thinks, *You are comparing me to the girl in the flick, and I don't measure up.* I've never fully understood why any woman with any measure of self-esteem would be willing to perform in front of a camera. But that's just the point. Her self-esteem has been trashed. And she's willing to trade any self-worth she has for money.

3. *Pornography creates abnormal expectations for satisfaction in marriage.* Once pornography becomes entrenched in someone's mind, what would normally satisfy in a loving relationship no longer is enough. Sex has to be kinkier, weirder, and often more unnatural and degrading.

4. *Pornography produces lust, which is different from strong passion or desire for the one God has brought into your life as your husband or wife.* God—not Satan—created sexual desire, and He made provision for it to be fully and completely satisfied in marriage! However, pornography cheapens the whole experience and produces lust, which then infects your

thinking and jades the way you look at every woman or man. Needed is the attitude of Job, who said, "I made a covenant with my eyes not to look lustfully at a girl" (Job 31:1).

5. *Pornography is addicting—just as much as drugs or alcohol.*

6. *Pornography is disturbing to children.* Don't kid yourself. Kids know what you have hidden in your lower chest of drawers or on your computer's hard drive. Viewing what you think is stimulating presents a disturbing, upsetting image to a child. It isn't the kind of sex education they need. A statement from the book of James says it all: "To him who knows to do good and does not do it, to him it is sin" (James 4:17 NKJV).

Re-ignite your sexual passion with each other. Is it wrong to have strong sexual feelings for the one you love, the one who committed himself to you at the marriage altar? The difference between lust and passion in marriage is that lust is directed toward someone you have no right to, whereas passion lights the flame that allows you to celebrate your love—something that is beautiful, pure, and wholly right.

Two passages of Scripture are often overlooked in this regard. In the New Testament book of Hebrews (a book that targeted primarily Jewish believers), there is a clear expression of God's approval. Literally the text says, "Marriage is honorable in every expression, and sexual intercourse is pure!" (Hebrews 13:4). The second passage is found in 1 Corinthians 7:1-4, where Paul stresses the responsibility that both husbands and wives have each to the other in meeting sexual needs because 1) we are sexual by nature, and 2) we live in a sex-saturated culture, very much as the Corinthians did long ago. Following a seminar my wife and I did on spouses meeting each other's needs in marriage, one woman expressed herself, saying, "I am so glad to know that what my husband and I have enjoyed doing with each other is not displeasing to God." The guilt that had distressed her was unfounded and misplaced.

If your love life is boring, get away for a weekend and rediscover what God intended to keep you caring and meeting each other's needs. Today, numerous books, including those from a Christian perspective readily found in Christian bookstores, help you to ignite your passion and break out of the blahs.

Guideline 3: Overcome boredom by discovering God's purpose and will for your life. Let's go back to some simple fundamentals for a moment. More than 20 million people have bought Rick Warren's book *The Purpose-Driven Life*. This demonstrates that the issue of existence— *Who am I? Why am I here on Planet Earth? And what lies beyond my last breath?*—has been one of paramount interest to people. The book begins with the statement "It's not about you." He continues, "The purpose of your life is far greater than your own personal fulfillment, your peace of mind, or even your happiness…If you want to know why you were placed on this planet, you must begin with God."[6]

Apart from God, life has little purpose or meaning. Out of the "no-God" vacuum developed existentialism, among other things, putting the emphasis on you and how you relate to the world. Absolutes have been tossed out, making truth subjective. Yet even agnostic Bertrand Russell acknowledged, "Unless you assume a God, the question of life's purpose is meaningless."[7] Even Moses, when he penned the opening statements of the book of Genesis (dealing with creation), made no attempt to prove God's existence. Writing, "In the beginning God…" assumed that reality. Until you find God, you begin at no beginning and work toward no end. No wonder people flatline emotionally when they leave God out of the complexity of the issues that confront them today.

We are also confronted with a pragmatic issue. How has this God revealed the purpose that is embodied in His will for our personal lives? Paul told the Philippians that he wanted to lay hold "of that for which Christ Jesus took hold of me," implying that God's purpose is not something unattainable or unknowable but something that can be discerned—a road map for life, a value system that safeguards relationships and provides meaning to existence.

A phrase that is often misunderstood—the will of God—is the outworking of what Rick Warren calls the purpose of God. Just as your father had a will for your life as you were growing up, so your heavenly Father has one for you that provides definition to the landscape of life.

That God should have a will for your life should be no harder for you to accept than the fact there is order and precision in nature itself. The planets are kept in their orbits by their precise relationship to other bodies, governed by the law of gravitation. The 23.5-degree tilt of the Earth on its axis is responsible for producing the seasons. And the intricacy of molecular structure gives order to life itself.

Now, if God has a will for these things, it should not be difficult to realize God also has a will for you. It becomes more apparent and personal when you come to Christ and receive Him as your personal Savior. Writing to Ephesian believers, Paul pointedly said, "Stop being ignorant, but understand what is God's will" (Ephesians 5:17, author's translation).

> A spiritual purpose in life eliminates the emptiness and weariness that drives men and women to the brink of suicide.

When Paul wrote to the Romans, he described God's will as "good" (the word means intrinsically good as opposed to something distasteful or repugnant), acceptable (understanding that God is a good God and that what He dictates for His children is in their best interest), and whole, or complete (fully satisfying).

It could very well be that your lack of emotional energy is caused from a lack of God-direction in life. You have no purpose, no goal in life, and you are uncertain of yourself and your destiny. You are cut off from God, and like someone who wanders through a desert in search of water, you wander aimlessly from one thing to another, searching and seeking but tired of it all. The result is boredom and fatigue. You are like an airplane pilot in a storm, searching for a landing field but unable to see anything at all.

In the pages of the Bible, we read of men and women whose lives were so very human. But whatever other difficulties they faced, their problem was never boredom. A spiritual purpose in life eliminates the emotional blahs that come to so many. With no sense of identity, no realization of why they are here, no goal of eternal destiny, people wander from one tasteless thrill to another, searching, seeking, but never quite finding. They never come to a knowledge of the truth.

In the biographies of outstanding Christian leaders—Martin Luther, John Wesley, John Calvin, Dwight L. Moody, George Mueller, R.A.

Torrey, and a host of others—you will discover that there were times when they were weary and tired from physical exhaustion, but they were never "bored" and without a sense of purpose in life.

Contrast that sense of purpose common to these leaders with the lives today of so many bored and apathetic individuals, people who are indifferent to life itself. Many people today have an abundance of material possessions, yet they are living in spiritual poverty.

A spiritual purpose in life eliminates the emptiness and weariness that drives men and women to the brink of suicide. If your boredom is because you have no spiritual purpose in life, do something about it. You need a God-connection with the One who loved you so much that He sent His only Son to Earth to speak to the needs of our lives and show us the way back to heaven. If you have already taken this step, get back into the center of God's will. That means doing His will from your heart—not out of a sense of duty, but passion. The very realization that God has a will for you gives life a sense of purpose. There is an ultimate destiny to your life, and it ceases to be an endless wandering.

Guideline 4: Displace boredom by realistically setting some goals for your life and home. "Where do you want Microsoft to take you today?" is the implication of the sales pitch for one of the most successful companies in the past half-century. Right? So ask yourself, "Where do I want God to take me today?" Wrong question. The issue is, "Who knows better where you need to go? You, or your heavenly Father, who knows the future, who knows what you need, and who will guide you to where He wants you to go, provided you trust His heart and follow Him?"

Recently I read where a business analyst reproved businessmen, charging that men set goals and have aspirations for their businesses, but when it comes to their families and personal lives, they have no plans or goals for the future at all. He charged that a lot of men don't know why they married their wives, nor do they know what they want out of life. And he is right!

Is goal-setting wrong? Not at all. If you don't know where you think God is taking you, you'll never get there, and that's why goals that are attainable, realistic, and flexible give you direction.

Goals for a family have to be a great deal more than material. They must also include qualities you want to see in the lives of your children and a plan as to how you can help them become the kind of young men and women you would like to see them become. Goals may include educational objectives as well as cultural and spiritual ones.

I am thinking of a young man who initially wanted to become a medical doctor, but he flunked out of college, the result of too much partying and too little studying. When he realized that his dreams and ambitions were fast slipping from his grasp, he went to a counselor, who spent time with him, helping him realign his goals and purposes in life, and motivated him to begin moving toward them. He went back to school and took a degree in biomedical engineering and found a job that was satisfying. What about you? When you fail, do you drag through life bored and defeated by this failure complex, or do you set new goals and begin to move toward them?

Guideline 5: Overcome boredom by injecting enthusiasm into your work. Our English word *enthusiasm* comes from two Greek words—*en* and *theos.* Thus *enthusiasm* literally means "in God."

She was known as "Teacher" to thousands of men and women. Among the most gifted and unusual persons I've ever met was Henrietta Mears, a great Christian educator. She was responsible for the establishment of Gospel Light Press, a well-known Christian publisher. She was also the inspiration behind the founding of Forest Home Christian Conference Center in California and a major influence in the life of Dr. Bill Bright, founder of Campus Crusade. She was a woman who majored in *enthusiasm,* and her brand was contagious. In fact, her friends referred to her as "Public Energy Number One."

I'll never forget the afternoon I met Miss Mears for the first time. I had just finished my master's degree and had a couple of weeks free. She had agreed to let me follow in her shadow for that time to see what made her tick. It didn't take long. Ethel Baldwin, her secretary, introduced me as I came into her simple, yet tasteful, office. With no ado, Dr. Mears briskly snapped, "Sit down, young man. In the next two hours, you're going to learn more about Christian education than you did all the time you were in school!" Like a machine gun firing bullets of enthusiasm, she was off and running!

That afternoon I did learn something that isn't terribly academic in nature, but it is vital if you are to succeed in life: If you don't have enthusiasm, you will never get yourself or your message across. In business, enthusiasm is the yeast that raises the dough. When you don't have a passion for what you are doing, no one else will get excited either.

Guideline 6: Break out of the morass of mediocrity. What's the opposite of boredom? Passion, enthusiasm, and excitement? Right. Vast numbers of people, some who rose from humble surroundings with no more probability for success than a man named Samuel Vauclain, have developed a passion for something—something bigger than themselves, something that not only changed their lives but also the lives of thousands of others.

You see, Sam was a lathe operator who had one of the dullest jobs in his company. Every day he stood at a machine and turned out bolts—about as exciting as watching the grass grow. He dreaded waking up each morning to face another endless day of standing in the same spot and doing the same thing over and over again. He wanted to quit, but jobs were hard to come by. He was afraid that if he quit, he wouldn't be able to find another job. In the meanwhile, he had a wife and kids to feed.

He felt like a prisoner, but since he couldn't quit, he began thinking of ways he could make a dull job interesting. "I've got it," he said one day as he had lunch with a fellow employee. "How about some competition with the rest of you?" Simply to break the boredom of doing the same thing every day, he began competing with some of the other lathe operators. What happened? His work started improving and the department's output increased—something that was not lost on management. That was the beginning of a series of promotions that eventually led Samuel Vauclain to the presidency of the very company for which he worked.

Is your job as boring as the one Sam had? Then what can you do to make it more interesting? Sometimes we are not as bored with our work as we are bored with ourselves. We keep looking for a new thrill, a new jolt, a new something for kicks, thinking that the problem is the environment—everybody else—when the real problem is internal. Remember the comic-strip character by the name of Pogo, whom I described in the preface to this book? His one-liner is right on target: "We have met the enemy and he is us!" When the problem is with you, a change of jobs will only produce temporary relief. Eventually, your new job will grow boring as well.

Guideline 7: Make a difference in our world. There are three levels of existence: 1) survival, 2) success, and 3) significance. Survival is where the majority of people live, work, and die. Their objective is enough bread for the day, and rarely do they break out of that existence. Some, however, through initiative, creativity, and hard work, become successful. They not only have enough for today, but they also have enough that they will never have need of anything money can buy. Often accomplishment by individuals in this group is not driven by need but by power and a sense of control.

Then there are those who come to a deeper understanding of what life's purpose is and attain the level of significance. They realize that what they have is a stewardship, placed in their hands by God Himself. Individuals in this elite group are driven by a passion to make a difference in our world. They consider their wealth to be something that is to be used for the betterment of humanity, not simply a commodity to be selfishly lavished upon themselves. They are the ones who build schools, hospitals, and orphanages, who provide the funding that combats HIV-AIDS and malaria—the number-one killer in Africa—and who spearhead ongoing cancer research and education, along with a list far longer than I could make. Their wealth crafts weapons that destroy poverty, ignorance, disease, and darkness in this broken world.

"Okay," you may say, "there are 60-watt bulbs, 100-watt ones, and massive spotlights that direct airplanes to the runways. I just don't happen to be a spotlight."

Then understand that God never holds you accountable for what you cannot do, for what you cannot give, or where you cannot go. But He holds you completely responsible for what you *can* do, for what you *can* give, and where you *can* go. How do you maximize your potential? How is passion generated for a cause that can change the world?

By dreaming? Not necessarily. While your dream may well be the faint impression of what God wants you to accomplish, dreams that are realized have to be incrementally translated into concrete and steel, and that is done by doing the small task as well as you can. Paul was driving at this when he wrote, "Whatever you do, work at it with all your heart, as working for the Lord, not for men" (Colossians 3:23). Paul had just given instructions to husbands, to wives, to children, and also to slaves, and he summarizes all of it with that advice. What he is really saying is, "Get with it! Don't go dragging through life. Whatever you do, do it with all your heart, as though you were doing it specifically for the Lord, and not for some other reason." Once you grasp this simple thought—or better yet, let this tremendous thought get hold of you—you will never be the same person. This concept puts enthusiasm in the dullest job. It lifts it right out of a boring setting and makes it come alive.

Paul wasn't the first person to sense this guidance from the Lord. A thousand years before, the writer of Ecclesiastes said,

> Whatever your hand finds to do, do it with all your might, for
> in the grave, where you are going, there is neither working nor
> planning nor knowledge nor wisdom (Ecclesiastes 9:10).

Here's how this truth can make a very practical difference. Several years ago, a charming, refined college professor came to me with a problem. She was one of the most gracious persons I had ever met. She had never married, and she had given herself totally to her work, gaining considerable prestige as the author of several mathematics textbooks that had a very wide circulation. Frankly, I was a little surprised to hear her unburden her heart.

She said, "I have a problem and I need help with it. I'm a terrible house-keeper and I know that it is not right, but I don't know what to do about it." Her life had been the classroom, and when she got home, she just wasn't interested in the proper end of a broom. Over many years, the magazines and books, along with her personal effects, had literally overflowed the closets and were stacked to the ceiling. We talked about the concept given to us in the words of Scripture, that we can face unpleasant tasks in life if we realize we are not doing it for any reason other than for the Lord.

What happened? Did it go in one ear and out the other? Not on your life! The first thing she did was to put a couple of college boys to work carting enough things out of the house to stock a thrift store. Boxes and boxes of discarded magazines and students' papers went to the dump. Gradually, the floors and closets began to reappear. She began to scrub and to scour, and her housework became not only bearable but likable.

The story I've shared with you won't be found in the introduction to the mathematics textbooks she has written, but believe me, it is the story of a life gripped with the concept that the most boring task can come alive when you take God into it.

Guideline 8: Search out the needs of others and give some of your time and talent to help someone less fortunate than you. Whenever Lillian Dickson, whose story was featured in *Readers' Digest,* spoke in the church I pastored, we always had to find something she could stand on. Her diminutive stature wouldn't let her see over the top of the pulpit. But dynamite, as they say, comes in small packages!

When her missionary husband died in Taiwan, everyone expected her to pack up and go home as most widows would have done. But not Lil Dickson. Instead of resigning herself to a life of boredom and ease, she rolled up her sleeves and accomplished far more than she ever did as the wife of a missionary and seminary professor.

Her efforts led to hospitals for the needy of Taiwan, clinics for leprosy patients, homes for unwed mothers, orphanages, and training centers for orphans and delinquent boys and girls. This remarkable woman traveled over rugged mountains establishing churches in primitive areas. Even when she was beyond the age at which most people retire, Lillian Dickson was full of life and energy. That word *boredom* was never part of her vocabulary. She was involved with the needs of others.

Apart from her dynamic outlook and can-do approach to problem solving, another thing that impressed me about this great woman was that she never wasted time on small talk. She also lacked the patience necessary to have clothes tailored for her, which was the way it was done in Taiwan then. Instead, she had every dress made from one pattern. Boring? Lacking style? Not to her! What was important to her was different from what counts with most people.

What about you? Have you learned that, from God's perspective, the small task in front of you is just as important as the big, glamorous one? Very few days are like the brilliance of a Roman candle. Life is filled with the commonplace and the mundane.

If you can sense the fact that there is a spiritual purpose when you are changing the linen on the beds or standing at the lathe and grinding out the same thing day after day after day, boredom will give way to meaning and purpose. Sometimes we are so close to the tasks of life that we just don't see the overall purpose in them. As the expression goes, we can't see the forest for the trees.

Guideline 9: Develop a passion to know God. Nobody ever really succeeds at anything for which he does not have passion. To make it to the top, there has to be a burning desire, a willingness to pay the price of hard work, loneliness, and study, and certainly a tough enough hide that what others think doesn't really matter. Whether your interest is collecting butterflies, doing medicine, making money, succeeding in a given sport, or living for God, without a passion for what you want to do, the flame goes out, and the journey becomes too arduous and difficult.

Uzziah became king in Israel at the age of 16 after the death of his father. He learned quickly and had a great heart for God. Says the writer of Chronicles about this man who reigned for 52 years,

> He did what was right in the eyes of the LORD, just as his father Amaziah had done. He sought God during the days of Zechariah, who instructed him in the fear of God. As long as he sought the LORD, God gave him success (2 Chronicles 26:4-5).

Simply put, this man had a passion for God, and as long as he did, God made him prosper. Question: Is the search for God endless? Does it become a maddening quest for something that can't really be achieved? Like climbing a mountain that has no peak, or running a race that never ends? Or reading a story which has no conclusion? Some think so. Long ago, however, God went on record, letting us know that when you make finding Him your passion, your desire will be satisfied. Says Jeremiah 29:13, "You will seek me and find me when you seek me with all your heart."

So what does that really mean? Okay, put it like this. You don't develop a passion for anything overnight. At first you are intrigued with something. It's a mild curiosity, but it is strong enough that you want to know more about it. Let's say, for example, that you are somewhat interested in photography. You admire beautiful pictures. But gradually your interest goes beyond just looking at photos taken by others and browsing through books about photography. You want to be involved personally. So you move from throwaway cameras to a good-quality digital one. You get better pictures. Then you want to edit your images, so you buy the software. You still don't know how to use it well, so you take a class.

But you don't stop at this level. You go to a photo exhibition and talk to a renowned photographer, who says, "Why don't you shoot some with me?" You are thrilled and become an understudy, learning from the artist who knows his stuff.

Frankly, developing a passion for God goes through the same steps. For many—perhaps for you—God is somewhat of an unknown curiosity, a kind of emotional security blanket to help get you through troubled times, but far from being a passion that consumes you.

Moving from slight acquaintance with Him to a level of personal knowledge means you begin to get involved in studies, and for the first time in your life you spend time in the Word. It begins to come alive. You understand it.

Don't stop there. Read men such as A.W. Tozer, C.S. Lewis, J.I. Packer, Oswald Chambers, and others. Better yet, spend time with mature brothers and sisters who have a passion for God, a burning desire to know Him and make Him known.

Someone who has a passion for birds never allows his detractors to keep him from the thrill of identifying a rare species or enjoying the sound of a meadowlark on a summer morning. Don't worry about what others think of your passion for God. Never forget that a fanatic is really someone who has a greater passion for God than you do.

A Postscript on Boredom

When I introduced the topic of this chapter, I used the analogy of what happens when a person's heart fails to function while that individual is connected to a heart monitor. The electronic pattern that follows the beating of a human heart flatlines. Alarms are sounded and people come running. I described individuals whose emotions flatline as boredom sets in (essentially the same thing in a different application), likening the process to what happens when a person stops breathing and life is gone. It is a kind of emotional rigor mortis!

There's one big difference, though. When a heart monitor flatlines, medical personnel apply 1400 volts of electrical stimulation to the patient— a real shocker, which jolts the heart into activity again. However, when you stifle your emotions and feelings, stuff them inside, and get so weary you don't have the energy to get excited about anything, usually nobody comes running to help you. No bells or alarms go off. You're on your own. If anyone does notice, that person generally walks away because you are no longer exciting to be around. You are dull—yes, boring!

> Jesus told us that He came to bring abundant life... That's what God wants you to have.

Have you heard the faint emotional beeps that are becoming more and more obvious, telling you that your emotions are starting to flatline? Listen to your heart. If you find yourself in the position I've just described, you need a jumpstart. You need reality to kick in and make you realize you are in trouble. You need help. Talk to someone—a counselor who gives you sound advice, a pastor who will listen and pray with you, a trusted friend.

Jesus told us that He came to bring abundant life—the kind that reflects love, joy, peace, longsuffering, gentleness, and kindness. That's what God wants you to have. Don't settle for anything less.

QUESTIONS FOR THOUGHT AND DISCUSSION

———— ✑ ————

Betty has worked as a receptionist for the same real-estate company for eight years. Every day she keeps a fresh pot of coffee brewing, and shuffles paper in between answering the phone. Every night when she gets home from the office, she complains to her daughter that her job is boring.

1. How might the boredom affect how Betty feels about herself and her role at the office? What can she do to make that job more interesting, provided she wants to keep it?

2. Think of a time in your life when you were bored for an extended period of time. What effect did that have on your energy level and your relationships? What steps did you take to get past that period—either to make the situation more interesting or to get out of the situation? Was there any permanent negative impact on your life or your relationships?

3. Name two activities that you feel are a waste of your time, insignificant but necessary responsibilities. What are three positive and important effects each of those activities has in your life or someone else's?

4. Get a piece of paper and divide it into three columns. Label one column My Job, another My Relationship(s), and the third My Fun. Write down three goals under each heading, no matter how basic or grand those goals might be, leaving space after each goal. Next, think through and write down what it will take to make those goals a reality. Then—and this is the hard part!—get to work on those steps!

This Will Hurt...

If you are bored, it will hurt to sit still and wallow in your boredom. God meant for our lives to be vital and productive. It will hurt to dwell on the negative aspects of the situation, and it will hurt to convince yourself that nothing will ever change.

This Will Help...

A *Peanuts* cartoon summed it up well when someone said, "We are overwhelmed with insurmountable opportunities!" If you are bored at work, start looking for the things that need to be done or ways that the situation can be improved. You might want to share your ideas with your boss. If you are bored in a friendship, talk with the other person about how you can bring the fun back in. If you are bored with yourself, travel, take a class, join a small group where you can interact with other people, start a new hobby, or do something you've always wanted to do.

Turning boredom into a challenge will help move you forward personally, professionally, or relationally.

CHAPTER 10

Coping with Stress

Which is easier to remember: the last time you reached for the bottle of aspirin and washed a couple down with a glass of water, or an afternoon of leisure when you had no agenda apart from what you wanted to do—a session with a good book, a quiet walk on the beach, or a stroll through the woods, where you drank in the smells of damp leaves and moss and enjoyed the beautiful wildflowers? That tension headache that made you snarl at your kids, grouch at your mate, and want to kick the cat didn't mean you had a brain tumor or needed to see a neurologist—it was a red flag as your nervous system screamed, "Help! I'm overloaded; I just can't handle this!"

You're not alone! Tension headaches regularly trouble as many as 100 million Americans every year, who go to doctors, who write 200 million prescriptions for tons of painkillers. The *New York Times Health Guide* says,

> Tension-type headaches are the most common headaches, accounting for nearly half of all headaches. According to one

study, nearly 40 percent of Americans have at least one epi-
sode of tension headache during the course of a year. Some
reports estimate that over 85 percent of women and about
63 percent of men will have a tension-type headache at some
point during the year.[1]

The problem is emotional overload, commonly known as stress. A
practical definition is that stress is "a state of physical and emotional
arousal caused by demands, pressures, and the wear and care of life."
You know what it is!

Stress is what you feel when...

- Your teenage daughter comes in and says, "Dad, you know
  that guy I met from Zambia? Well, we're going to elope!"

- There is too much month left at the end of your money.

- You are late for a flight and learn that the next plane arrives
  after the wedding.

- You look in the rearview mirror and see a red light flashing.

- Your husband gets passed over for promotion.

- Your rich aunt dies and you find out you've been cut out
  of the will.

- It's the week before Thanksgiving and you are the turkey!

Everybody knows what it is: the businessman trying to make a profit
in a down market; the salesman who tries to reach his quota and earn
the big bonus when his goal seems always to be just a step ahead of him;
the single parent who tries to be cook and bottle-washer, chauffeur, and
mom and dad, and keep his or her own act together; the college student
facing the keen pressure of competition; the medical professional who
tries to meet the needs of patients on the graveyard shift when half the
staff didn't even bother to call in sick.

Let's personalize it. Finish this sentence:

STRESS IS WHAT I FEEL WHEN_____!

Then take a few minutes to evaluate your stress level.

Dr. Hans Selye was one of the modern pioneers of investigating stress and stress management. He is credited with inventing the term itself, borrowing it from physics to describe the body's response to a wide variety of emotions and physical experiences.[2] Born in Vienna, he came to the U.S., where he entered medical school at the prodigious Johns Hopkins School of Medicine. He eventually went to McGill University in Montreal, where he began his life work as professor and director of the Department of Experimental Medicine and Surgery. This widely acclaimed endocrinologist did more work on the subject of stress and received greater accolades than any other twentieth-century scientist. He wrote more than 33 books and 1600 articles on the subject. Selye, who died in 1982, didn't believe that our present generation faced more stress today than did previous generations, including the "Greatest Generation" of World War 2. But he did believe that we are not handling it as well.

If, however, the letters and e-mails that come to our office each week as the result of broadcasting on 1000-plus radio stations are any barometer of what is happening to us today, I think it is fair to say that we are facing greater stress than grandfather ever imagined in his worst nightmare, and also that we handle it less capably than he did.

Researchers are telling us that stress is doing everything from producing cancer to lowering the IQ of our children.

Not All Stress Is Bad

- Stress causes the tension that holds the suspension bridge up over the raging waters.
- Stress on the drum head allows the instrument to resonate to the beat of the drummer.
- Stress on the strings of the violin allows the bow to glide across it, producing a beautiful melody.
- Stress motivates you to find a solution to a problem.

Some individuals actually thrive on stress! The goalie in soccer's World Cup goes out on the field knowing that success or failure may depend on his frantic leap to stop or deflect the ball from the net, yet neither his mother, the apostle Paul, nor an angel from heaven could stop him from going out there. He's determined to go for it! And so may you!

Professional athletes will tell you that they play better, are sharper emotionally, and are more concentrated when they have competition.

A lot of folks actually perform better, sell more convincingly, and rise to greater levels of accomplishment when they are under a certain amount of stress. But too much stress causes the suspension bridge to collapse, the string of the violin to snap, and the drum head to burst. And stress can kill you.

What Excessive Stress Does

When you are confronted with a stressful situation, it takes only 15 seconds for the hypothalamus gland in your brain to trigger a burst of adrenaline, which begins to surge through your veins, kicking in what psychologists describe as the fight-or-flight syndrome.

1. Stress affects your emotions. A rainbow of emotional response may be triggered, ranging in scope and intensity from overt anger to fear, and when you are under prolonged stress, your emotional responses, which are normally pretty cool and measured, become strained. You become irritable and cross and probably say things you don't really mean and do things you later regret. It is usually members of your family and those who are closest to you who become the victims of your stress.

Most arguments in a family take place within 30 minutes of the dinner hour, usually when a family member comes home under stress and says or does what he couldn't get away with on the job. Stress produces in you the disposition of a junkyard dog who is cruising for a fight.

Under stress, our emotions can affect us in ways that are counterproductive to accomplishing what we want to do. Take, for example, the following situation. "United flight cancelled when pilot says he's too upset to fly," read the caption that appeared in *USA Today.* The pilot had been seen in a heated conversation on his cell phone at the gate, saying he "was going to complain to the union." After the passengers were seated he made an announcement that he was too upset to safely take the passengers to their destination. "The passengers reacted to the pilot's announcement with a collective groan," reported Roger Yu.[3] Wouldn't you have done the same thing, even though you were glad he hadn't risked your life because he had blown an emotional fuse?

2. Stress affects your body. Take your fist and double it up for a full minute as you read the rest of this page. Before you finish you'll notice that your fist begins to throb. God didn't intend you to walk around with your hand tensed as a lethal weapon. Yet when you are under stress, you stomach begins to knot just like your fist, and you can't tell it, "Hey, stomach, just relax!" So you have your "Maalox moments" as you try to calm your nerves.

Jane Brody, writing for the *New York Times Guide to Personal Health*, says,

> When most people talk about stress, they mean the negative reactions: a churning gut, aching back, tight throat, rapid heartbeat, elevated blood pressure, mental depression, short temper, crying jags, insomnia, impotence, viral infections, asthma attacks, ulcers, heart disease, or cancer.[4]

In chapter 3 I wrote about the link between strong negative emotions such as hate and resentment, and cancer. Consider the following:

- Carolyn Poirot writes in the *Fort Worth Star-Telegram*, "Studies confirm stress is often at heart of cardiac risk... New studies published in separate journals of the American Heart Association have come up with the numbers to prove what we knew deep in our hearts all along: Emotional and psychological stressors, especially depression and anxiety, are bad for our health."[5]

- A study at Duke University demonstrated that those who learn to handle stress reduce their risk of a heart attack or significant heart problem by 74 percent.

- "Research suggests a biological link between psychiatric health [and the] likelihood of cancer," says an Associated Press release quoting Dr. Redford Williams, based on studies done by four researchers at Ohio State University's College of Medicine.[6]

Another seldom-considered side effect of stress is that it not only makes you look older, it actually causes your body to age. Here's why. Stress physically affects your body's chromosomes and causes the tiny caps on the cells' chromosomes that govern cell regeneration to get smaller. When the tiny caps get too short, the cells stop dividing and eventually die.[7]

3. Stress also affects your spiritual life. When you are under stress, you feel you are doing something wrong. God seems distant and remote. You feel guilty about feeling the way you do, and this gives rise to two myths, two misconceptions, which haunt you:

- Myth 1: Christians shouldn't face stress.
- Myth 2: Those who do are not spiritual!

The editor of a Christian magazine heard one of my radio programs dealing with the subject, on which I said (quoting John Powell), "When you repress your emotions, your stomach keeps score." She wrote me,

> This was your voice followed in a brief minute by your praying for strength for those struggling with this problem. To which I replied, "Praise the Lord" and cried. Yesterday I was told by my physician that there is a strong possibility that I have an ulcer. I must go in Monday for tests to try and determine this or discover what other possibility it might be. This sets hard with me, as in my opinion ulcers and Christians should not go together. I equate this with a lack of dependence on God.[8]

Should you feel as our friend did, ponder this for a minute. In your living room is an end table, which was designed to support a lamp or a vase and a few trinkets or magazines. Used for the purpose for which it was designed, it handles the weight adequately. Now, suppose you need to put up new drapes and hate to bother getting the ladder out of the garage. You take a look at the table and think, *I can stand on that!* and pull it over to the window.

Chances are that it may wobble a bit, but it holds your weight! But you can't quite reach the top of the drapes, so you call your husband, who is watching TV, and he comes to your assistance. If both of you stand on that table, it will probably collapse under the weight.

It's perfectly obvious that the table is not spiritual, right?

Wrong!

Spirituality has nothing to do with the issue. The table didn't come from the drawing board of the designer to be used as a ladder. You violated the purpose for which it was created.

You have emotional load limits, and when you carry greater burdens than our Designer ever intended you to bear, your spirituality is not the primary issue—your load limit is.

To think that believers in Jesus Christ shouldn't face the consequences of stress is about as realistic as saying that Christians should never have colds or the flu. But the way you as a Christian perceive stressful circumstances has a great deal to do with how you cope with them. Says Hans Selye,

> Attitude determines whether we perceive any experience as pleasant or unpleasant, and adopting the right one can convert a negative stress into a positive one.[9]

Actually, there are situations when a person's stress level is appreciably increased because of his faith. Take, for example, the woman who wants to take her children to church on Sunday morning, when her husband would much prefer her company preparing breakfast or being at home. Besides, her going to church makes him feel guilty, which only increases his irritability, which in turn creates higher stress levels.

Scores of people can readily testify to the fact that fellow employees know of their faith and, not sharing those convictions, make comments that create stress.

God's People in Scripture Who Experienced Stress

Here's Daniel in the lion's den. He knows that if his prayers don't reach heaven fast, he's on the menu for breakfast—terminal stress, as I view it.

Remember Esther? Convinced that there is only one way she can save her people, the Jews, she is determined to risk her life going before the king. "If I perish, I perish!" she cries. That's stress, any way you define it.

Consider the stress Joseph faced. He was falsely accused, wrongly convicted of sexual assault, and thrown into prison. Knowing that most men would have succumbed to the advances of Potiphar's wife, Joseph could have thought, *God, is this what I get for playing it straight?* There is no record that he felt "put upon" by the Almighty, but you can be sure he felt stress—to which any person can testify who has ever known the despair of hearing the key turn in the jail door.

> If they had given Olympic gold medals in stress, surely the apostle Paul would have won one.

Elijah knew stress as he watched the waters in the Brook Cherith dry up—as perhaps your finances have done.

Anyone who has ever taken a tour group to Israel and tried to satisfy the whims of such a group of people, many of whom have never traveled abroad, knows in a very, very small way the stress Moses experienced as he tried to keep two-and-a-half million people satisfied.

David knew stress. Anointed by Samuel to be king, he watched the months turned into years as he became a fugitive from the angry fits of Saul, who didn't want to relinquish his throne. For seven long years David fled for his life, finally seeking refuge with the enemies of Israel, the Philistines.

If they had given Olympic gold medals in stress, surely the apostle Paul would have won one. Take as an illustration the stress he experienced on his second missionary journey.

It began when Paul had an argument with his best friend, Barnabas.

Barnabas: "Let's take John Mark on this trip!"

Paul: "No way, Barney! Remember, he chickened out and quit on us on the last trip!"

Barnabas: "If he doesn't go, I don't go!"

And he didn't!

That was stressful!

Taking Silas, Paul journeyed to Troas, where he planned on turning east into Bithynia (north-central Turkey today), but God closed the door. Anyone who has had a trip interrupted by delays or visa rejection knows the stress it creates.

Turning west, Paul and Silas ended up in a prison in Philippi, with their feet in stocks and their backs burning from the stripes that were unjustly laid on them.

Yet Paul could write to the Corinthians,

> We are hard pressed on every side, but not crushed; perplexed, but not in despair; persecuted, but not abandoned; struck down, but not destroyed (2 Corinthians 4:8-9).

In the Upper Room, when the cross was looming on the horizon, Jesus told the disciples: "I have told you these things, so that in me you may have peace. In this world you will have trouble. But take heart! I have overcome the world" (John 16:33). The Greek word translated "trouble" also means difficulty, or pressure, and stress is the inevitable consequence!

What Are the Sources of Stress

Dr. Jack Morris notes five major sources that create stress today:

1. change
2. conflicts
3. criticism
4. concern (anxiety or worry)
5. compression

At times more than one of these gets to you. You can probably relate to the following:

> My job keeps me under a lot of pressure because I am in a managerial position. I have made two home moves and one office move in nine months, my boss was transferred to another department, and thus I must adjust to new management. I now must supervise a full-time assistant (for me a new experience). I am heavily involved in my church (often four evenings a week), and so there have been a lot of pressures...so I worry about that, the stomach gets more upset, more worry, a vicious circle.

You can't totally escape it. You can usually only trade one gunnysack of stress for another, which contains a different pattern but is essentially the same.

Three young executives on Wall Street discovered this fact the hard way. Tired of the stress and pressure they experienced in the New York brokerage firm where they worked, they decided to liquidate their assets, buy a sailboat, and relax as they sailed around the world.

Great idea!

The sailboat was equipped, and their journey was begun. In a few months they sailed into one of the most beautiful lagoons they had ever seen. Miles of beautiful, undulating sandy beaches, clear blue water, beautiful coral reefs, and warm, romantic breezes.

"What a magnificent place for a resort!" one of them commented after a few days of enjoying the scenic beauty.

"Yeah, that's what I've been thinking," replied a second.

In due time they decided to stay and build that resort. The contractor was hired, but the local contractor worked on a native schedule, not on a Western one. Materials couldn't be located, deadlines were ignored, and nobody was upset—apart from the three men who wanted to put the resort together.

When it was finally finished, they discovered that the locals weren't terribly interested in arriving at work on time or in getting messages to the resort (no cell phones!) when they couldn't work.

One set of stressful problems had been traded for another!

Coping with stressful events magazine-style. Articles on stress and how to cope with it have proliferated like weeds in an unkept garden. Get on a plane and the airline magazine is almost certain to have an article for travelers on stress management. Push your grocery cart to the check stand and you are greeted with magazines with headlines in bold type that scream, "You can put stress to rest in your life!"

I've read a lot of them, and most of them leave you with a feeling of hollowness or even frustration. Like a mother's kiss on a child's skinned knee, they may help for a bit, but the uplift is temporary and more like a desensitizer than a real cure. It seems to me that there are many variations of three basic themes:

1. *Alter or change your perception of a stressful situation.* This may be one of many ways that help you put the situation that bothers you into perspective.

2. *Practice relaxation techniques.* Visualize a beautiful meadow with snowcapped mountain crests behind and a stream meandering through the lovely flowers. Try listening to soothing music. Discover deep breathing. A variety of visual stimuli all fit into this category. Get exercise—jog, swim, bicycle, walk, do aerobics. And so forth.

3. *Medicate the problem.* Tons of tranquilizers either work on the central nervous system or allow tense muscles to relax, decreasing the level of stress.

All of the above may be helpful, but is there no more than this? Does the child of God who takes seriously the instruction of Scripture have additional tools available with which he can cope with stress? Or are we pretty much on our own?

Insights from Scripture That Enable You to Fight Stress

Guideline 1: Get God's perspective. To do this it may be necessary for you to back off from the stressful situation and put both it and God in perspective. We are often so close to whatever is creating stress that we see neither God nor the problem in its true perspective. Stress seems to shut God out from our lives.

Go out and look at the stars on a dark night and realize that the closest star is Alpha Centauri, 26 trillion miles from Earth. Light from that star, traveling at the speed of 186,400 miles per second, still takes about 4.5 years to reach us.

Look at the magnificent Milky Way spread across the heavens, and tell yourself that before God ever created the first star and put in it the sky, He knew about the stressful situation that confronts you right now.

When tomorrow comes, God will be there to welcome you. Nothing takes Him by surprise.

In the days when computers ran under DOS and had a CPM operating system, I placed a line in the startup routine of my computer that read, "REMEMBER, THIS TOO SHALL PASS." Every time I booted the computer, it stared me in the face—a simple, brief reminder that helped me put things in their proper perspective.

Quite often we lose sight of the fact that much of what is so important today will be of little significance ten years or perhaps even ten days from now. We exhaust a hundred dollars worth of adrenaline on ten-cent events and people.

A sign reads,

RULES FOR STRESS:
1. *Don't sweat the small stuff.*
2. *It's all small stuff.*

Sure, you can fight back. You can tell 'em off. You can file a grievance. You can let your temper flare and tell them where to go. Does it really matter that much?

Gaining God's perspective enables you to view the circumstances in a different light when you are the child of God. The Bible says that nothing happens to His children as a matter of chance or fate.

Paul wrote,

> In him [Christ] we were also chosen, having been predestined according to the plan of him who works out everything in conformity with the purpose of his will (Ephesians 1:11).

And to this great truth add the comfort of Romans 8:28: "We know that in all things God works for the good of those who love him, who have been called according to his purpose."

The events that create stress are tools in the hands of God, and the circumstances that appear so hostile may actually be allowed by a loving God because He wants to accomplish something lasting and worthwhile that would never happen apart from your being in the pressure cooker.

One more thing must be said. There are times when this point of view must be taken by faith. When you can't see His hand, you must trust His heart. Circumstances seem to defy what I've just written. Then you have to tell your doubts where to get off and hold on to the truth you know but may not feel. In the midst of a stressful situation you can't see the end—only God can. But when you are convinced that God is a good God, you can hold on and trust Him, which brings us to the next step.

Guideline 2: Let your relationship with God be an anchor that holds you steady in the time of storm. The writer of Hebrews in the New Testament says that our faith is "an anchor for the soul, firm and secure" (Hebrews 6:19). The analogy is that of a ship that is not at the mercy of the storm because it is held safely by an anchor that will not fail—much like the individual who has assurance that there is more to life than what he makes of it. He is not at the mercy of the circumstances.

When you are trusting the Lord to bring order out of the chaos that brings stress, you will feel the effect of the storm, yet you will not drift and be destroyed by the rocks.

Frankly, God never even suggested that sufficient faith would eliminate stress in our lives. He said,

> *When* you pass through the waters, I will be with you; and
> *when* you pass through the rivers, they will not sweep over
> you. *When* you walk through the fire, you will not be burned;
> the flames will not set you ablaze (Isaiah 43:2).

Notice that God never said, "If you should happen to go through the waters, fire, or flood." He said you *would* go through them. Similarly, Jesus was emphatic in saying, "In the world you will have trouble," but the promise of His presence in times of stress becomes an anchor that gives strength to face the realities of life.

When you were a kid, did you ever face off with rowdy kids in your neighborhood and exchange words? Perhaps standing on your side of the curb, you hollered, "My daddy can beat up your daddy!" and then ran for home.

Why not try that in relation to the stressful event that has robbed you of peace of mind? Do you really believe that your heavenly Father is sovereign Lord and God of the Universe, that He is stronger than the forces of evil that have perhaps brought stress to your life? Why not hurl those words at the circumstances and then head home and get on your knees and remind God that you are His child and that He promised to never leave or forsake you? (See Hebrews 13:5 and Matthew 28:20.)

An acquaintance of mine will put his feet on his desk and say, "So what if they fire me. They can't take my family, they can't take away my wife or my children. All they can take is my paycheck, and I'll trust God for my needs as Scripture says I can, so I'm not going to worry."

Guideline 3: Stop bearing your load and God's as well. Worry says in effect, "God, you aren't big enough to handle this situation, so I had better figure out what I'm going to do!" Do you really think that God went back to heaven, closed the door, and left you to fend for yourself? If not, then realize that there are times when you have to say, "Lord, I can't handle this. It's bigger than I am. There is absolutely nothing I can do about it—so you take over!"

Nothing creates greater frustration than not being able to solve our own problems. Problem-solvers by nature, we want to work out the solution, but often life presents us with circumstances we cannot change: an illness, a difficult situation with a boss, a young adult child who seems to be making a decision he will later regret.

Guideline 4: Apply scriptural principles to the situation creating your stress. If your stress is the result of conflict with someone—either you have a gripe with someone or another person has something against you—you can probably relieve much of that stress by taking courage in hand and confronting the individual (see Matthew 16:12,14-15). Confrontation, stressful as it may be initially, can be positive and eventually eliminate much of the turmoil you have lived with in the past.

At the age of 71, Dr. Hans Selye was interviewed and asked very personal questions about his life and what his research had demonstrated. In relation to the stress of conflict with other people, he said,

> I find that I cannot carry grudges. If wronged by some friend or colleague, I may break off contact out of sheer self-protection, but I bear him little enmity. After all, nature gives even the most fortunate of us only a limited capital of energy to resist stress, and it would be silly to squander it on anger.[10]

Affairs, dishonesty, deceit, and a host of other practices that the Bible catalogues as sin create stress—both in the life of the individual who practices them, and certainly in the lives of those who are part of his family. As I've noted before, James 4:17 says, "To him who knows to do good and does not do it, to him it is sin" (NKJV). Pretty blunt? Right!

Guideline 5: Decide what your physical and emotional load limits are. No two individuals have the same physical strength. One hunk of a man may bench-press 300 pounds, while another can't handle 50. One just happens to possess a physique the other doesn't have. Naturally we would all prefer to look like the chiseled-V specimen, but because we possess different DNA and can develop our natural potential only so much, that doesn't mean, for a moment, that one is of less value or considered more important than the other in God's sight.

Likewise some individuals have an amazing resiliency and can cope with vast amounts of stress quite well. Others can handle very little. How much you can handle is something that only you can decide.

Samuel Plimsoll (1824–1898) convinced the British Parliament to enact legislation that required a line to be placed on the hull of every British ship so that cargo could be loaded only to the point where the Plimsoll line (as it came to be known) met the water level. Loading a ship beyond that point, which had been done often by greedy shipowners, had jeopardized the lives of the sailors as the ship was tossed by an angry storm. No wonder this gentleman was known as the sailor's friend.

But you aren't born with that line! Your boss isn't going to decide when you've had enough. Your husband or wife can't say when. Your doctor can't. You are the only one in the entire world who can say, "Enough!"

Learning to say "No!" is one of the most difficult things we have to do. Why? We want to please people. We want people to like us, so we often end up saying "Yes" when we would like to say "No," but we just don't have the courage to do it.

If you are among those I've just described, you can do what I have to do on occasion: Say, "I'd like to say 'yes,' but it's just not possible. I've made a previous commitment." (That previous commitment may be to your wife or to yourself—a commitment to keep your sanity.)

Guideline 6: Budget stress by managing your time. There is much inequality in life! Whoever said life is fair? One person can eat anything he wants. The other walks by a bakery and just smells the delicious odor of gooey cinnamon rolls and gains weight.

But when it comes to time, gifted or neglected, rich or poor, young or old, in prison or free, every person has exactly the same amount: 168 hours to the week, 60 minutes to the hour.

Much of our everyday stress—though certainly not all—is the result of poor time management. We procrastinate. We put off doing the necessary. The tyranny of the urgent saps our hours, and what we really needed to accomplish never gets done. Of course, if I fool around doing last-minute e-mail and don't watch the clock and face rush-hour traffic between my home and the airport where I am to catch an international flight, I'm going to get uptight and stressed out. I have no one to blame but myself in that situation. I can tell you by personal experience that I've found it far less stressful to give myself gap time, arriving well in advance of a flight and spending an hour sipping Starbucks, than to fight traffic to make the flight.

If you need some simple help in getting a handle on your schedule, what I'm about to describe will work, provided you work it.

1. Take a blank sheet of paper, or a tablet, and divide it into three columns that you label MUST DO, SHOULD DO, CAN DO.

2. Then under the MUST DO heading, make a list of everything that has to be done without fail this week. Then number the items, listing the most important one first, the next most important as number two, and so forth.

3. In the list of SHOULD DO items, put tasks of secondary importance—perhaps items that need to be done next week but aren't really urgent or pressing.

4. The CAN DO list includes items that will eventually need your attention, and as time passes those items may move from right to left as they gain importance.

5. Now, go to work on that number-one item on your MUST DO list. Though you are tempted to avoid that phone call because you don't especially want to talk to that person,

don't put it off. Do the most important one first, and don't go on to the next item until you have finished that task.

Does it work? You will be amazed how much stress you can eliminate by prioritizing your pressing tasks and then doing the most important task first.

Guideline 7: Be filled with the Spirit of God. Without going into a long theological discourse, let me give you a picture that will help you see this point. First, understand that when you became a believer in Jesus Christ, God's Holy Spirit came to indwell your heart and life (Romans 8:9).

Paul also gave us a command, a straightforward admonition to "be filled with the Spirit" (Ephesians 5:18). At the risk of oversimplification, this means, let Jesus Christ be Lord of your life and ask Him to take control: guiding you; helping you draw from Him the resources of grace and strength you lack; and helping you trust Him to work His will in your life as you do your part to the extent you know how by following His will that is revealed in Scripture. Wow! All of that! Oswald Chambers put it in three words: "Let God engineer!" In other words, you willingly invite Him to take control of your life.

> The potter placed one hand within the vessel and with the other hand applied pressure from without.

In Paul's second letter to the Corinthians, he writes,

> We have this treasure in jars of clay to show that this all-surpassing power is from God and not from us. We are hard pressed on every side, but not crushed; perplexed, but not in despair; persecuted, but not abandoned; struck down, but not destroyed (2 Corinthians 4:7-9).

That's a picture of a person who faces stress—plenty of it—but is able to handle it. The secret? The indwelling presence of God's Spirit, who makes up for what you lack.

Again, picture three vessels or vases: One made of clay, another made of marble (stronger), and one made of stainless steel. Obviously, their ability to withstand stress is in increasing order. Now, in your mind's eye, picture a strong hand within the weaker ones that equalizes their strength and gives all three the same ability to withstand pressure from without. Getting the picture? That is exactly what the Holy Spirit will do in our lives.

When I was a boy growing up in Colorado, I remember visiting Van Briggle Pottery in Colorado Springs. I watched with interest as an old potter took a lump of clay, kneaded it with his hand, molding and shaping the lump. Then he put it on the potter's wheel as he began working the treadle with his foot.

From this amorphous lump of clay, slowly the shape of a vessel began to emerge. Carefully the potter placed one hand within the vessel and with the other hand applied pressure from without in order to shape the vessel he was making.

There is the hand of God within you which will support you; and without, the strong hand of the Almighty likewise ensures that nothing beyond His power will ever confront you.

His strength within is more than equal to the stress without.

QUESTIONS FOR THOUGHT AND DISCUSSION

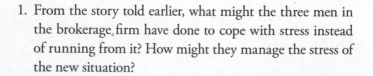

1. From the story told earlier, what might the three men in the brokerage firm have done to cope with stress instead of running from it? How might they manage the stress of the new situation?

2. Think of a time when you were under a lot of stress. What effects did it have on you and in your life? How did you manage—or not manage—the pressure and its impact?

3. What are three good stresses in your life? What are three bad stresses? What steps can you take today to keep those things in balance instead of letting them overwhelm you?

This Will Hurt…

Sometimes we think that being under stress means that we settle in for the long haul and keep pushing through. It will hurt if you think of taking breaks as *weakness*. It will hurt to convince yourself that you can rest later—after the deadline is met, on the weekend, after the kids are grown, when you retire.

This Will Help…

Evaluate whether the stress you are facing is the positive kind that helps motivate you to accomplish things, or the negative kind that pulverizes your productivity. Learn to work *smarter*, not *harder*, whether the task is cleaning the house or winning an account. We all need to take care of ourselves physically, emotionally, and spiritually. It will help to consciously focus on ways to do that each day.

CHAPTER 11

Burnout—Terminal Stress

For generations parents told their children, "Nobody ever died from hard work—now get out there and go to work!" But that is no longer true. Behavioral scientists began using a term to describe people, a term that was formerly used of engines that had exhausted their fuel: BURNOUT. Burnout is what happens when a person works too hard, under too much stress, for too long a period of time, causing him to lose his equilibrium. It has been defined as "failure or exhaustion because of excessive demands on energy, strength, or resources."[1]

Dr. Carolyn Karr, Associate Professor of Social Studies at Marshall University, writes,

> There are more people in danger of succumbing to the burnout syndrome than in any period in our history. The reasons are quite simple: There are more people working; there is greater competition for existing jobs; and inflation is placing tremendous pressure on people to keep the jobs they now have.[2]

What Kind of People Burn Out?

The people who are especially vulnerable to burnout are those in highly stressful situations and professions. Burnout describes people who once loved their work but who are now overwhelmed by it. They no longer cope effectively. It's not that they can't—it's just that they have lost their desire to cope. Burnout is the most severe form of stress, and it can be terminal.

With computers, MP3 players, e-mail, instant messaging, cell phones, and a vast array of electronic devices that are supposed to simply life, the reality is that life has become more complex. Consider the following:

- One third of us feel "rushed" all of the time.

- Office workers receive an average of 170 messages every day.

- Sleep deprivation is common. The average person sleeps two-and-a-half fewer hours each night than people did 150 years ago.[3]

- According to *Medical News Today,* up to 70 percent of Americans experience trouble sleeping due to anxiety, depression, and stress.[4]

- The equivalent of five years of the average life span is spent waiting.

Is it any wonder that our stress levels are challenged?

The formula for burnout is simple:

PEOPLE-TO-PEOPLE CONTACT + STRESS = BURNOUT

According to Herbert J. Freudenberger, a New York psychoanalyst and author of the book *The High Cost of High Achievement,* certain personality types are more prone to burnout than others.[5] They include the following:

1. *The person who needs to succeed and feel successful.* Often this person has come from a rather insignificant social background. Perhaps he has risen through the ranks from the

bottom. He may be from a very poor family, and becoming a person of status is very important. Winning is the name of the game for this type of person; it is the only thing that really counts.

2. *The overcommitted individual.* Ministers, missionaries, and church workers step to the front in this category. Does that mean that their commitment to God is too great? No, but it may mean that their commitment to His work is, and that they have difficulty distinguishing between the two. Bearing loads of responsibility that God never intended them to bear, they eventually want to walk away from the whole thing, "throwing the baby out with the bath water," as it were.

3. *The extremely competent individual.* This type of person thinks he is the only one capable of handling the job. You get the feeling he actually considers himself indispensable. This person has usually never learned to delegate responsibility, and when he does he often ends up taking back the very task he assigned to someone else. When this pattern is at work, there is a burnout candidate in the making.

Burnout: A New Outbreak of an Old Disease

Burnout isn't new. You can read about it in the pages of the Bible, where centuries ago individuals such as Jonah (the one who had the encounter with the great fish) and Elijah (the fiery prophet who did combat with the priests of Baal but ran from a woman whose name was Jezebel) were confronted with it. I think we face it in greater measure today, however, than previous generations. People who should by all rights be productive become warped, exhausted, and—well, burnt out. Knowing the symptoms and being familiar with the stages of the burnout process can help you avoid this fate. You don't have to be a casualty.

Burnout will affect all three of the areas that make up your life: the physical, the emotional, and the spiritual. Although, as we previously discussed, the three cannot be separated into neat little compartments, there are, nonetheless, very definite symptoms in each.

Physical symptoms. Physical weariness is one of the most prominent symptoms. When you are faced with burnout, you are tired all the time. You go to bed tired, you get up tired, you run tired all day. In fact, you even sleep tired. You traipse from meeting to meeting, from appointment to appointment, from event to event. Whereas you used to get excited and enjoy people, you are now bored and apathetic.

You may also suffer from any combination of the following: headache, gastrointestinal problems, weight fluctuation—generally weight loss, but it can be the opposite—insomnia, hypertension, and even chest pains. These are not imagined symptoms; they are very real. Like the engine that has exhausted its fuel, you are rapidly exhausting the physical, spiritual, and emotional resources that make life vibrant and meaningful.

Emotional symptoms. Burnout causes dramatic changes in personality. Outgoing, extroverted people who customarily make significant contributions to meetings and in discussions with their associates can become quiet, withdrawn, and even sullen. The burnout candidate who used to have energy for romps with the kids and household chores is listless and lethargic. He's lost interest in everything. A person who has been pretty much under control becomes irritable and often hostile. He may be depressed. He tends to be rigid and wants to make no changes. Any question is interpreted as a challenge, and your suggestion is considered insubordination.

Spiritual symptoms. The burnout candidate feels that God has become remote, uninterested, and distant. He becomes critical of fellow Christians. He loses interest in the Bible, and when he does read it, which is rather seldom, it makes little sense. The pages merely contain printed words, not a message from God. He has no time for personal prayer unless it is a frantic cry, "God, if You're there, help me to get through this mess." Church attendance becomes perfunctory, if he even continues to go at all. When he does attend, he doesn't see much right. He fidgets like a kid sitting in the corner and can't wait to get out of there. Instead of listening, he's miles away, wrestling with issues that seem to be overwhelming.

The Four Phases of the Burnout Process

It is generally recognized that there are four phases to burnout, and the passage from one to the next is not always clearly designated with a sign that reads, "You are now leaving stage 2 of the burnout process!" There is no flashing sign that blinks in large letters: "You have entered the critical phase and are about to burn out!"

These phases and their characteristics are as follows:

	Phase 1 Challenge	Phase 2 Commitment	Phase 3 Containment	Phase 4 Collapse
Characteristics	• Goal-oriented • High expectations • Idealistic • An achiever • Determined	• Life still adventurous • "Thrill of the kill" • Building • Productive • Achieving	• Workaholic • Pursued by goals • Driven • Feelings of being unappreciated • A warped perspective • Physical, mental, and emotional exhaustion • Sensitive and combative	• Overwhelmed • Shame and doubt • Quits or escapes • May use drugs, sex, or excessive alcohol • Broken relationships • Fellowship with God is strained • Family and close friends are alienated

What the phases look like. When a person begins any new thing in life—a new job, a business, a challenge, or a project, he is usually excited about the possibilities in front of him. He is full of idealism and eager to pour himself into the task. As time goes on, however, a person passes into the second phase. This, too, is generally a productive stage. His work still is exciting, and he is still reaching forward in a spirit of adventure. This stage is a building phase. There is satisfaction in seeing accomplishment. He is pleased that hard work and initiative pay off.

Gradually, however, the pace of life accelerates. His day planner entries or his schedule on his handheld becomes more crowded. Leisure and relaxation are almost nonexistent. That's when a person is no longer pursuing his goals; rather, his goals pursue him. Life in phase 3 is like the downhill run of an 18-wheeler that has lost its brakes. The line between phases 3 and 4 is blurred—he's going too fast to see that things are out of control.

The burnout candidate in phase 3 is not quite out of the game, but he is only one short step away, as when there are two strikes against the batter and the pitcher is winding up with a fastball. This person feels unappreciated. He develops a martyr complex. He's caught in the firm jaws of a stress trap that is slowly squeezing the life out of his existence. He can relate to the saying, "The hurrier I go, the behinder I get"; he feels like he just can't get on top of things. He ends up hurting the very people he wants to help.

An article in a nursing magazine summed up the situation in that context:

> You entered nursing to help people...to do good for humanity...
> then one day, you're ashamed because you yelled at a patient.
> On another day you cry over the cruelty of death. You slip
> into days of avoiding patients...or even making fun of patients'
> personalities or illnesses. You begin to dread work. You become
> cynical—and you're ashamed of yourself for feeling that way.
> You become disgusted.[6]

One morning, the burnt-out person wakes up and says to himself, *Is this all there is to life? It just isn't worth it! I'm out of here!* The trap has squeezed hope out of him! He's in the fourth stage of the cycle. He may simply walk out, slam the door on life, quit. He has gradually become overwhelmed by what should have been a satisfying and fulfilling career. He despairs and desperately wants to escape; drugs, alcohol, even sexual encounters are enticing diversions from reality. Those who are closest to the person are usually the ones who get hurt in the explosion. "This is not the man I married," is a common complaint, or "She's married to her work—not me!" Relationships are almost always strained or broken. And then...

- The neurosurgeon quits practicing medicine and sells real estate.

- A pilot walks off the flight and says, "I'm through," and becomes a nature guide.

- A female executive says, "They can have it," and opens a hair salon.

- A Christian leader resigns and begins a recycling business.

- A nurse in a coronary unit quits and starts a flower business.

Mark Gorkin, known as "The Stress Doctor," says,

> One of the reasons the fourth stage is so disorienting is that a person's psychological defenses have worn down. Cracks start appearing in the defensive armor. Painful memories and old hurts normally contained by your emotional defenses are leaking through the cracks. A slight or emotional bump can set off an overly sensitive and personal reaction. Now a mate's occasional, somewhat annoying behavior really irritates as it reminds you of a mannerism of your father. Or jealousy towards a colleague reeks of sibling rivalry.[7]

A huge phenomenon. When I broadcast a series of programs about burnout on my radio program, *Guidelines,* we received the greatest response that has ever come to our office in more than four decades (with the possible exception of a series of programs we released on depression). One woman described phase 4 in these words:

> My husband got up from the dinner table one Sunday evening in January, and left us. He sounds so much like the person you described in your three programs this week. There isn't anything I can do about him because I don't know where he is.

The following are very typical of other letters we received:

> Your description of the burnout victim sounds exactly like my wife who works as an assistant manager in a bank...In fact, she suffers from every one you mentioned.

> I've come to the shocking realization that you have depicted my life to a T. My wife is a reading consultant for neurologically impaired children while I am a communications manager for a large company. Both of us have had it!

What You Never Learned in an MBA Program

1. **Even spiritual giants burn out!** You can read in the Bible of Elijah's traumatic burnout. Here was a prophet who single-handedly confronted the 450 prophets of Baal (1 Kings 18–19), but the emotional and physical drain resulting from the confrontation of this man of God with the false prophets brought him to the brink of burnout. When he was challenged by Queen Jezebel, he gave in to the exhaustion, and he turned and fled for his life.

The life of Elijah reminds us that even spiritual giants get tired and discouraged. No wonder James, the half brother of Jesus, some 700 years later wrote, "Elijah was as completely human as we are" (James 5:17 MSG). Even the most godly people are susceptible to burnout. Just because you think you are indispensable, God won't cut you a deal and give you super-human strength.

2. **Even nature teaches the importance of restoration.** A period of rest and restoration always follows the harvest. Winter always follows autumn. This is God's way of allowing the land to replenish itself. Constant production without restoration depletes the natural resources and diminishes the quality of your life. There is no time for what you once enjoyed. You've forgotten how to play, to have fun or relax.

3. **Jesus and all of the Scriptures clearly teach that rest is critical.** When the 70 who had been commissioned by Jesus to minister in nearby cities returned, Jesus instructed, "Come apart and rest a while."

And the apostle Paul recognized that burnout is a grave threat to those involved in people-to-people ministries. He instructed, "Let us not become weary in doing good, for at the proper time we will reap a harvest if we do not give up" (Galatians 6:9). The King James Bible puts it a bit more succinctly: "In due season we shall reap, if we faint not." In today's language, Paul might say, "We will eventually accomplish our goals if we don't burn out first."

4. **What you are in God's sight—your character, integrity, faithfulness, and commitment to values—is more important than what you accomplish.** "Dad was a Phi Beta Kappa, a Rhodes Scholar, and a company president," remarked a young man, adding, "but he flunked marriage, fatherhood, friendship, and fun." Having lost sight of God's perspective, the burnout candidate feels that accomplishment is the only thing that counts. He usually places greater value on his goals than on people, so reaching his objective is the only thing that matters. The goal may be a good one in and of itself; the problem is with how the goal is accomplished.

> "It is better to burn out than rust out," some people say...I don't think God would have us do either.

The *Wall Street Journal* in conjunction with the Gallup organization surveyed the heads of 780 major corporations, focusing on work habits and attitudes and how they coped with the pressures in relationship to their marriages and their children. The survey was based on interviews with 360 CEOs among the 1300 largest corporations. It included 100 of the Fortune 500 companies—276 heads of medium-size companies, and 198 independent owners of small businesses.

And how are these leaders coping with success? Here's the bottom line:

> The survey delivers an unmistakable verdict: home and family come second for the typical corporate executive...Among the specific findings: chief executives typically work sixty to seventy hours a week, travel six to ten days a month and give up many of their weekends for business meetings.[8]

Having made it to the top, two out of every three executives said they were convinced the pressures were greater and the cost to their family more severe than when they were middle managers. One company president quipped, "I gave my family everything in the world but myself."

When a person faces burnout, no matter what field he's in, the person's family is always affected. More times than not, his marriage is seriously threatened in the process. A person can leave behind a great organization and a legacy of admirable benevolence. But if he burns out in the process, if his family has to pay the price, it's not worth it. If you can head off burnout before it has done its deadly damage, the later years of your life will be happier and far more productive.

"It is better to burn out than rust out," some people say. In one sense, they may be right. But I don't believe we're supposed to choose the lesser of two evils. I don't think God would have us do either. The Bible describes ways we can reach our goals without burning out.

Walking Away from the Brink and Gaining What Really Counts

Suppose you are driving down the highway in your car and the red light on your instrument panel indicates that your oil pressure is down. The engine still sounds good. When you gun the throttle, it responds normally. What do you do? You can either continue driving and ignore the light, or you can pull over, investigate, and determine what is wrong. Even if you choose to ignore the warning light, your automobile will continue to perform for a while just as it always has. But eventually you'll find yourself at the side of the road with smoke pouring out from under the hood of your car. You are finished—at least for the moment!

What do you do when you see the signals, the warning indications that you have moved from the commitment stage of life to the containment stage? Do you ignore the signs, or do you do something about them? It is one thing to recognize the symptoms; it is another thing to know what to do about them. And it is entirely another matter to be motivated enough to take action, to come to a place where you say, "Enough is enough! I will do something about my life to ensure I don't become a burnout victim!" Again, your wife can't do it for you; your husband can't do it for you. Only you can.

When I delivered a series of lectures in Australia that focused on the problem of burnout, especially among professionals involved in Christian work, a participant at the conference came to me afterward and said, "There is one more stage to the burnout cycle, which you have overlooked!"

"What is that?" I asked.

"It is *comeback*," replied the friend.

He's absolutely right! Individuals who have burned out don't have to quit forever, and they don't have to use burnout as a rationale to excuse their behavior. Through restoration and healing, there is a way out of collapse. One woman described her comeback like this:

> About three years ago I experienced burnout myself and am just now putting myself back together. My husband and I came very close to becoming separated...but something beautiful has come of it. With three children, ages thirteen, eleven, and two, I am very glad with the enormous help of God, we put things back together again. Your program and tapes have been a great deal responsible for our marriage and sanity's survival.

The habit patterns that led to burnout in the first place will challenge restoration and healing, but you can come back. As you begin to reverse some of those well-worn habits, the inner struggles that have torn apart the fabric of your life will begin to subside, and peace will flood your heart. It is well worth the sacrifice and determination. When you are challenged with burnout, remember, you *can* make a comeback. The following guidelines will help you regain your footing and, hopefully, find healing, restoration, and renewal in your relationships, your marriage, and your faith.

Guideline 1: Get your perspective right. Jesus did not heal everyone in Palestine when He was here on Earth. Undoubtedly, there were many people within easy walking distance who had needs—deep needs—and Jesus didn't get to them to minister to them. There were limitations to what even He could accomplish in the flesh and still maintain His spiritual life.

You can't bear the burdens of the entire corporation, or even your own department, organization, or church. Therefore, if you are to avoid burnout, you have to bring your priorities into subjection to the will of your heavenly Father. What is it that God wants you to do? Decide what the *main thing* is and make it just that. When you take more upon your shoulders than God intended you to, you will spread yourself too thin, and some of your tasks will not be done as well as they could have been.

Part of restoration is confronting your denial, acknowledging that you were totally consumed, confessing your imbalance and failures to those close to you, and turning your ambition toward new, more realistic goals.

This means reprogramming the computer that drives you! Does this mean lowering your goals and expectations? Perhaps. But it demands that they be brought into sync with reality. Better to settle for less and have your sanity, your marriage, and your self-respect than to try to have it all and end up playing the fool who loses everything.

In her book *Having It All, Having Enough,* psychologist Deborah Lee quotes an investment consultant as saying, "Having both work and family is a plus." She points out that a balanced portfolio is much safer than having all your stock in one company. Question: "Can you really have it all?" Can you have a rewarding job and a happy family—a high-powered, high-stress job with a lot of demands and a salary to match at the same time you are a mother or a dad who is there for his or her children? Can you succeed in business and still be there when your child takes his first step or throws his first ball at Little League? Can you sit on the corporate board and be there for Parents' Day, when your daughter's first-grade teacher shows moms and dads how well little Teresa can read?

Can you have it all? Before you really decide, give your heart a listening ear. Balancing home and family responsibilities with business requires the skill of a diamond cutter and the balance of a tightrope walker. Knowing when to prioritize, of course, is the key to the whole matter. But I, for one, am convinced that it is impossible to have it all and to do it all. There are just not enough hours in a day, nor is there enough emotional energy to measure up to the unrealistic expectations that society, the workplace, and our consciences place upon us.

This demands tough decisions as to what is important in your life, especially in the long run. Of course there will always be specific needs in both the workplace and our social lives that demand extra hours and energies, but deciding what is important and then making long-range decisions in light of those major goals helps you to decide where to draw the line—when to say, "I'm sorry, but my answer is no."

I always say, "Hurray!" for the person with the courage to place long-term values ahead of short-term accomplishments—which may mean turning down the executive position to have more time for the children, or saying "No" to the job offer that requires a major move away from family and your support group.

A word of warning: Affirming long-term values comes at the cost of short-term losses. Okay, you may not get the promotion or the pay increase or the special bonus, but you do live without as much stress and may, perhaps, see your child take his first step and be there when your son hits the ball out of the park or receives his honor for excellence at school. Surely that counts for something.

If you continue to strive to have it all, you're going to end up with either a very guilty conscience or a first-class case of burnout. That's why you've got to decide what is important and then make the hard decisions.

One of the reasons it is so difficult for us to come to terms with this issue is that we have lost sight of what really counts, including being a mother or a dad. Long ago we forgot that the hand that rocks the cradle is the hand that rules the world. The few brief years of parenting are quickly over, but our failures as parents carry into the next generation.

Picking up the phone, I heard the voice of my youngest daughter, who somewhat tensely said, "Dad, I've got five minutes to get stuff out of the house before the fire is so close I have to evacuate. What should I take?" I thought for a moment and said, "First get the kids and the pets, grab your financial stuff—jerk the cables out of your computer and throw it in—and then grab the pictures of the family off the wall and beat it!"

She did! By God's provision, the fire stopped at the road. Talking about the challenging situation later, Nancy said, "It was rather shocking to me that there was so little in our house that really counted for anything once I had my children and a few pictures and financial records and had escaped unscathed!"

"Having it all" is an oxymoron—a kind of contradiction of terms. It's what you really want that will eventually determine what you get. Yes, life is a matter of balance, but like the juggler who has crystal balls in the air, which won't bounce off the pavement, you must realize there are no second chances, no returns to "Go" on the Monopoly board of your life. That's why careful, prayerful decisions will produce long-range dividends. Get real. Forget about having it all and decide what is really important in your life, and make that your priority.

Guideline 2: Mend your fences. Saying, "Okay, I'm back," won't cut it. You will have to re-establish relationships, something that is difficult but not impossible. Almost always when an individual has pushed the envelope and the stress has pushed him or her toward the brink, it is a given that relational damage has been done to the family. Your mate, your kids, as well as close friends, have been alienated and wounded.

The following illustrates the damage that is often done when an individual burns out and the victims include his children. At a conference I spoke of a Christian leader as a man of leadership and compassion. I pointed out that the organization that he founded had touched the lives of thousands of children around the world. After I had finished, a woman approached me. As she began to speak, her voice was tense with emotion. She asked, "Did you really know [and she mentioned the name of the man I had spoken of]?" Wondering where the conversation was going, I somewhat hesitantly replied, "Yes, I think so."

"You didn't know him like I did," she said. "I was Sharon's best friend." And then I knew why she was angry. Sharon, the daughter of the man who had done so much for so many children in the world, had, sadly, taken her life in her late teen years.

As a torrent of intense, angry words poured out, she told me how she had been in that home when the dad came back from overseas trips, physically and emotionally exhausted—burned out—and transferred those uncontrolled emotions to his wife and children, who paid the price for his stretching himself so thin.

You need to start with your marriage. Instead of doing what most burnout victims do, which is to say, "Hey, what's the use? Let's just call it quits," you need to convince your mate that you still care, that you want to rebuild, and that you believe there can be flowers after the fire. Saying this isn't going to convince your spouse, but showing it day by day will finally convey that message.

It will be equally challenging in a different way to reestablish relationships with your children who, frankly, may not be terribly excited about having you back in their lives. They learned to live without you quite well, so taking you back into their lives and schedules may not happen immediately.

How do you convince a skeptical wife or husband that you deserve another chance? What does it take to be a promise keeper? What does it take to be there for your kids? It takes the conscious, determined decision that your spouse and children are more important than your work, your love of sports, or your misplaced preoccupation with success. And you are the only one in the world who can demonstrate that.

Guideline 3: Take time off. You must learn to take time off for rest and recuperation. That includes spiritual recuperation as well. "There is no music in a rest," wrote a famous composer, "but there is the making of it." When your Internet connection goes down and you become distraught, or you can't have an evening without your cell phone ringing a half-dozen times, or you can't carry on a conversation with your spouse without thumbing your handheld, you're in trouble.

Turn off your cell phone and answering machine. Set time limits within which you will do e-mail and surf the Net. Learn to laugh again, to relax and have fun. Attitudes are conveyed nonverbally, and when you take your youngster to a ball game or a concert but wish you were back at the office or at your computer, you send a nonverbal message: "You really don't count for much!" You don't say it. But the message gets through loud and clear.

When Dan's business failed, he was burned out, and he knew it. Wisely he borrowed money and escaped, taking his wife to Hawaii for two weeks. Sitting on the beach, talking together, and working through his disappointment was one of the best things he could ever have done. He got in touch with his emotions and feelings, and his wife saw a side of him that had been hidden for a long time. And out of this came a business plan that did succeed.

Guideline 4: Start taking care of yourself physically. This doesn't mean that you should stand in front of the mirror longer, applying your makeup or combing your thinning hair. What it does mean is that you need to stop neglecting your body. Most people who are on the verge of burnout have been so busy that they have had no time for tennis, jogging, or any other physical exercise. They are usually overweight. Instead of exercise, they turn to the refrigerator. They run up a flight of stairs and are out of breath for an hour.

Your body is the temple of the Holy Spirit, and you need to start taking care of it. This involves a combination of proper diet, exercise, and recreation. You're not a machine that can be programmed; you are a person created in the image of God. You have a human body, which is God's property, and it must be given proper care. In chapter 3 I talked about getting in touch with your emotions, which means stripping away the calloused, hardened layers of repression and allowing the fragrance of a rose to reach your nostrils, the smile of a baby to warm your heart, and the warmth of your lover's hand to raise your temperature. When you've become as stiff as a corpse, it's time for a resurrection.

Guideline 5: Learn to say "No!" Earlier in this chapter, we discussed a personality type, a person who has to do everything himself. This person, in the early stages of the game, may think that there are two kinds of people, the willing and the able—but he believes the willing are not able and the able are not willing. Thus he personally takes on more and more responsibilities to ensure that the job gets done and objectives are accomplished. After all, the needs he's meeting are real, and "no" is a word he has never learned.

Any person, however, needs to know when to use that word, whether or not he is the type who cannot delegate. The good is the enemy of the best. We all need to learn to say more often, "I would very much like to take on that responsibility, but with my present commitments, it is impossible. Thank you very much, but my answer is 'No.'"

Life is a matter of choices. Not all of those choices are between good and bad. Each of us must evaluate several good things and then choose the best. Sometimes those choices become difficult. Life is often a compromise between what you would like to do and what you can do.

Guideline 6: Delegate responsibility. This means at home as well as at the office. Of course you can do the job better than the person to whom you delegate the task; that's probably why you are in charge. But being in charge also means being able to delegate, and being able to delegate means yielding authority to the other person so he can get the job done.

Once you've delegated something, turn loose. Don't attempt to micromanage the person. Give them the same latitude to get the job done that you had coming up through the ranks. In the words of Dwight L. Moody, "The successful man isn't the man who does the work of ten men, but the man who gets ten men to do the work."

Guideline 7: Learn the secret of spiritual renewal. If there is a secret to spiritual survival, it is this: Your relationship to God through Jesus Christ must be sustained on a daily basis. That relationship is never a one-shot-for-life sort of thing. It involves a vibrant life interaction with a living Savior. Paul wrote,

> We do not lose heart. Though outwardly we are wasting away, *yet inwardly we are being renewed day by day* (2 Corinthians 4:16).

Daily renewal involves quiet reflection and time with God. I find it works best to start your day reading His Word and opening your heart to Him in prayer. When I get to the place where reading the Word is mechanical and perfunctory, when I go through the motions but don't get anything out of it, or I pray and it seems that the heavens are brass, I recognize this as a danger signal. It is a red light flashing on the instrument panel of my spiritual life that says, "You're going too fast, man—slow down!"

Reading God's Word aloud may help. Pray as you walk through your neighborhood or a park. Join a small group where you can talk about your needs and new commitment to both God and your family. Journal, recording your thoughts, as you embark on a new phase of your life.

Guideline 8: Make God laugh. "If you want to make God laugh," says a bumper sticker, "make plans!" And what is the real message—that you should never try to plan anything? No. Rather, when God has been left out of your plan, you may never reach the finish line and the gold cup (or gold watch and retirement speech). There's a better way. Submit your agenda to Him, realizing that burning out is never pleasing to Him. His plan is for you to finish the race and finish well! Submitting to His will means that when things don't always go according to your plan, you stop long enough to take inventory and find out where He is leading you.

Whether you climb a mountain, traverse an ocean, build a house or a high-rise building, run in the Olympics, or attempt to plant a garden—or for that matter, do about anything—there are scores of factors over which you have little, if any, control. Like what? Like the economy, the weather, the availability of goods and services, the flow of electrical current that can wipe out machinery, the capriciousness of trade and surpluses, and a host of other things. The fact is, there are a lot of factors we take for granted over which we have very little control. Does this mean that we should sit on our hands, waiting for God to make things happen? Not unless you are expecting a new outpouring of manna from heaven. God honors planning and hard work, but what makes God laugh is the presumption that men and women often have, which ignores Him entirely.

> Want to make God laugh? Then make plans and leave Him out of your plans.

Take, for example, the Babylonian king Nebuchadnezzar, one of the most powerful men who ever lived, who was the dread and fear of all the earth. He's the one Daniel tells about whose heart was filled with pride. God finally said, "Enough!" The king's mind snapped and he "ate grass like cattle. And his body was drenched with the dew of heaven, until he acknowledged that the Most High God is sovereign over the kingdoms of men and sets over them anyone he wishes," wrote Daniel (see Daniel 5:21).

Several generations ago, Christians often signed their letters using two Latin words, *Deo volente,* which means, "God willing." They recognized that God—not chance or fate—is the final arbiter of what happens to us in life.

Presumption is a sin that God detests. Want to make God laugh? Then make plans and leave Him out of your plans. Apparently this is not simply a problem that we who are living in the twenty-first century struggle with. It's an old one. James, the half brother of Jesus, wrote about this very situation when he penned the letter that bears his name—which, incidentally, was probably the first New Testament book. He wrote to Jewish Christians—probably merchants—and said,

> Now listen, you who say, "Today or tomorrow we will go to this or that city, spend a year there, carry on business and make money." Why, you do not even know what will happen tomorrow. What is your life? You are a mist that appears for a little while and then vanishes. Instead, you ought to say, "If it is the Lord's will, we will live and do this or that." As it is, you boast and brag. All such boasting is evil (James 4:13-16).

How could it be any plainer?

Guideline 9: Learn to live for the moment and make today count. My friend Wayne Pederson used to sign his letters and e-mails with the words "Focus forward!" No more. He's changed the closing to read, "Seize today!" He discovered that when he was always focused forward, pushing to reach goals and objectives, he missed a lot of the view on the journey. Wayne came to the conclusion that he was so focused on what he wanted to see happen in the future that he was missing what was happening today. He confessed what a lot of us should admit. "When I go running," he said, "instead of enjoying the fresh air, the sights, and the exercise, I find myself thinking, 'I can't wait until this is over.'"

Waiting for a flight, he picked up a book at the airport by Spencer Johnson entitled *The Present*. Says this popular business-oriented author,

> When you receive the present, you no longer spend your time dreaming about being somewhere else. You're intent only on what's happening at that moment. It means focusing on what is happening right now.

And when all of this came together, Wayne began to realize that it was time to make some personal adjustments and change his focus from *forward* to *today!* You can do the same thing. *Today counts—seize it!*

When you seize the moment, you enjoy the happy chatter of children playing, notice that roses still smell, sense that the hand of your sweetheart is soft and tender, and laugh! And when you laugh, God will smile!

QUESTIONS FOR THOUGHT AND DISCUSSION

———————————∽∂∾———————————

Brad graduated with an MBA, one of the top students in his class. He started climbing the corporate ladder and became just as successful in his profession as he was in school. He has all of the toys that go along with success—the BMW, the Rolex, a membership in an elite country club—and all the marks of a man who is going somewhere. He also has a wife and two young boys, and is on four committees at church—and is the chairman of one of them. He feels good about his life, but he is tired a lot of the time, and evening meetings cause him to miss his sons' baseball games quite often. Recently he has been skipping lunch because he doesn't feel like eating, and muscle spasms in his lower back are getting to be more than occasional.

1. What are some of the obvious signs that Brad may be a burn-out candidate? Each person can handle a different amount of stress and number of commitments. If Brad wants to maintain a very high level of quality activity, what are some of the things he needs to put into practice?

2. Hard work is a good thing. What was one time when you let hard work get out of balance? How did you bring it back into balance so it was a creative instead of a destructive force in your life?

3. Consider the four phases of the burnout cycle: challenge, commitment, containment, and collapse. Which phase are you in—at work, at home, personally? What are some things you can do today to move into the comeback stage?

4. We have discussed a number of stress-related issues in this book. What is a specific stress point you have that we did not talk about? How might you use some of the information in this book to help?

5. Do you honestly see yourself in the burnout phase? If so, what positive steps will you take to alleviate the stress in your life? Write them down. Talk about them with your mate or associates.

This Will Hurt...

Many people believe that the only way to have the lifestyle they want is to give in to excessive hard work. It will hurt if you justify your choices based on material rewards. A BMW, as too many people find out, will not keep a marriage together. It will hurt to keep pushing, driven by the sense that making it big is a demonstration of your worth. It will hurt to ignore the red lights on the dashboard of your life.

This Will Help...

Know yourself (chapter 1) and what characteristics contribute to your being a candidate for burnout. It will help to set your priorities so you can balance all of your responsibilities. Occasionally give yourself permission to let something fall by the wayside—without feeling guilty!

A Final Word

A grandfather who saw considerable action in the War would sit out on the porch with his grandsons and entertain them with stories of his valor. One warm Sunday afternoon, he recounted one of his favorite stories. He had carried the flag for his regiment, and though the bullets were flying all around him, he gained the crest of the hill and proudly planted the flag in full view of the enemy.

After he finished the story, he sat back, expecting the children to say, "Hey, that was great, Grandpa—tell us another story!" Instead, one of the boys asked pensively, "But Grandpa, what happened?"

That's the question I want to leave with you as we come to the end of our discussion of how you can make your emotions work for you. What is going to be different in your life as the result of reading this book? What decisions have you made that must be executed? Where do you go from here?

You are the one who holds the answer. Today can be different from yesterday because God is the God of the present. He wants to meet you at the point of your deepest need.

God gave you emotions to make your life bright and beautiful—not dark and dingy. Make friends of them. God is fair, but life is not! That's why, living in a broken world, you will never control what happens to you or what other individuals do to you. Life is an ongoing challenge, which means you will continue to face challenges. You are the one who must decide whether you react to them or respond to them.

Remember, no one can force you to choose hate, anger, or rage! I am absolutely convinced, however, that much of what robs us of peace and wholeness is contrary to God's plan and purpose for our lives. You can make friends of your emotions and allow them to work for you. In so doing, you can discover your potential to be all that God created you to be. May God help you to do so!

If I can be of personal help, I would be happy to hear from you. You can write to me at the following addresses:

In the United States write to

Guidelines

Box G

Laguna Hills, CA 92654

In Asia write to

Guidelines

Box 4000

Makati City MM, Philippines

E-mail sent to **guidelines@guidelines.org**
reaches me anywhere.

For additional resources,
visit our Web site at **www.guidelines.org.**

Notes

Chapter 1: Understand Yourself—You're Worth the Bother

1. David Ferrell, "The Brain: An Inner Universe," The *Orange County Register,* July 1983, J, 11. For further information, see Neal Miller, "Start at the Top: The Brain Is Our Giant Data Base," The *Orange County Register,* June 12, 1985, D1.

2. Laura Krauss Calenberg, "The Search for Lasting Beauty," www.everystudent.com/features/beauty.html.

3. Soren Kierkegaard, *Works of Love,* tr. David Swenson, as quoted by Cecil Osborne, *The Art of Understanding Yourself* (Grand Rapids, MI: Zondervan, 1967), 217.

4. Joshua Liebman, *Peace of Mind* (New York: Simon and Schuster, 1946), 71.

5. As reported by Andrew Blankstein and Ari B. Bloomekatz, *Los Angeles Times,* June 17, 2008, 1.

Chapter 2: Answering the Question—*Who Am I?*

1. John R.W. Stott, "Am I supposed to love myself or hate myself?" *Christianity Today,* April 20, 1984, 26, italics added.

Chapter 3: Making Your Emotions Work for You

1. James Drever, *Dictionary of Psychology,* as quoted by A.W. Tozer, *That Incredible Christian* (Harrisburg, PA: Christian Publications, Inc., 1964), 49.

2. "Emotions likened to primary colors," http://en.wickipedia,org/wiki/Emotions.

3. *Macbeth,* act 2, scene 2.

4. Bruce Narramore, "Learning from the Emotional Life of Jesus," www.ncfliving.org/jesus_jesus/emotions.php.

5. S.I. McMillen, *None of These Diseases* (Old Tappan, NJ: Fleming H. Revell Company, 1964), 15.

6. Viktor Frankl, *Man's Search for Meaning* (New York: Washington Square Press, 1968), 213-214.

7. John Schindler, *How to Live 365 Days a Year* (Old Tappan, NJ: Prentice Hall, 1954).

8. Michelle B. Riba, "Cancer and Emotions: Is it Normal to be Depressed?" *Cancer News,* www.cancernews.com/articles/cancer&depression.htm, June 24, 2008.

9. Frankl, *Man's Search.*

Chapter 4: Making Friends of Your Emotions

1. "Women more likely than men to put emotions in motion," www.vanderbilt.edu/News/news/june98/nr4.html.

2. Freda Petersen, "Women's emotional responses 'wired in,'" www.smh.com.ar/articles/2002/07/23/1027332379838.html, June 24, 2008.

3. A.W. Tozer, *That Incredible Christian* (Harrisburg, PA: Christian Publications, Inc., 1964), 49.

4. Matthew Elliott, *Feel—The Power of Listening to your Heart* (Carol Stream, IL: Tyndale House, 2008), 103.

5. Elliott, *Feel,* 130.

Chapter 5: Memories That Burn

1. James L. McGaugh, as quoted by Jerry Adler, *Newsweek,* May 19, 2008.

Chapter 6: Anger—Friend or Foe?

1. James Comer, "How To Control Your Anger," *U.S. News and World Report,* October 1977, 53. Also see "Millions May Have Rage Disorder," www.webmd.com/news/20060605/study.

2. Robert C. Larson with Neil C. Warren, "You can be Angry and still be Good," *Moody Monthly,* December 1975, 49.

3. Comer, "How to Control."

4. Leo Maddow, *Anger,* as quoted by Larson, "You Can Be Angry," 51.

5. Josette Mondanaro, as quoted by Peggy Eastman, "I'm So Angry I Could Die!" *Vital,* 1981, 45.

6. Eastman, 41.

Chapter 7: The Inner Struggle of Worry

1. Paul Meyers, *The Log of the Good Ship Grace* magazine, September 1972, 1.

2. Clovis Chappell, *Questions Jesus Asked,* as quoted by James Hewett, *Illustrations Unlimited* (Wheaton, IL: Tyndale House, 1988), 496.

Chapter 8: Winning the Battle with Fear

1. George S. Patton, as quoted by Bob Kelly, *Worth Repeating* (Grand Rapids, MI: Kregel, 2003), 120.

2. Millard Sall, "Why Am I Afraid?" *Decision,* November 1980, 8.

3. George Sweeting, *Who Said That?* (Chicago: Moody Press, 1995), 196.

4. Sweeting, *Who Said That?,* 196.

5. Harold J. Sala, *Today Can Be Different* (Ventura, CA: Regal Books, 1988), July 17.

6. F. Wilbur Gingrich, *Lexicon of the Greek New Testament* (Chicago: The University of Chicago Press, 1965), 230.

7. Gingrich, *Lexicon,* 230.

8. Craig Massey, "When Fear Threatens," *Moody Monthly*, September 1970, 20.

9. Harold J. Sala, *Coffee Cup Counseling* (Nashville: Thomas Nelson Publishers, 1989), 146.

10. David Maraniss, *Rome 1960—The Olympics that Changed the World* (New York: Simon & Schuster, 2008), 151.

11. Thomas Butts, "Tigers in the Dark" as told by James S. Hewett, *Illustrations Unlimited* (Wheaton, IL: Tyndale House Publishers, 1969), 205.

12. http://en.wikipedia.org/wki/New_England's_Dark_Day.

Chapter 9: Boredom—When Your Emotions Flatline

1. Betty Friedan, *The Feminine Mystique* (New York: W.W. Norton and Co., 2001).

2. Harry Johnson, "That Tired Feeling—Its Cause and Cure," *Reader's Digest*, October 1966, 142-143.

3. Steven Winn, "We Try Our Best to Avoid It but Boredom Has Its Benefits," www.sfgate.com/cgi-bin/article/cgi/?f=c/a/2004/04/02/DDGHJ5UGM51.DTL.

4. A. Dixon Weatherhead, *Family Circle*, November 1965, 137.

5. "That Tired Feeling," *Family Circle*, November 1965, 137.

6. Rick Warren, *The Purpose-Driven Life* (Grand Rapids: Zondervan, 2002), 17.

7. As quoted in Warren, *Purpose-Driven Life*, 17.

Chapter 10: Coping with Stress

1. "Tension Headache," *New York Times, Guide to Personal Health*, June 25, 2008, 1, www.health.nytimes.com/health/guides/disease/tension-headache/risk-factors.html.

2. Hans Selye, as interviewed by Laurence Cherry, "Straight Talk About Stress," *Readers' Digest*, June 1982, 145.

3. Roger Yu, *USA Today*, June 28, 2008, 3B.

4. Jane Brody, *New York Times Guide to Personal Health*.

5. Carolyn Poirot, *Fort Worth Star-Telegram*, as quoted in *The Register*, November 12, 1997, 1.

6. *The Register*, "Research...," May 27, 1984, A21.

7. Sarah Mahoney, "10 Secrets of a Good, Long Life," *AARP Magazine*, July-August 2005, 66.

8. For many years it was commonly believed that ulcers were the result of worry or disturbed emotions. However, ulcers may be the result of H. pylori bacteria and can usually be effectively treated with antibiotics. On the personal note, I've been there and done that!

9. Selye, "Straight Talk," 146.

10. Selye, "Straight Talk," 147.

Chapter 11: Burnout—Terminal Stress

1. Herbert J. Freudenberger, "Psychotherapy: Theory, Research & Practice," Spr. vol. 12, 73-82, http://psycnet.apa.org/index.cfm?fa=main.doiLanding&uid=1976-10574-001.

2. Carolyn Karr, as quoted by Donna Sammons, "Burn-out," *Family Weekly,* March 9, 1980, 15.

3. Richard A. Swenson, "The Epidemic of 'Overload,'" *Decision,* February 2000, 9.

4. www.medicalnewstoday.com/articles/12742.php.

5. Herbert J. Freudenberger, as quoted by Sammons in "Burn-out," 15.

6. Cheryl Pilate, "People-orientated Professionals Risk Burnout," *Register,* February 26, 1981, E-11.

7. Mark Gorkin, "The Four Stages of Burnout," www.stressdoc.com/four_stages_burnout .htm.

8. The *Wall Street Journal,* date unkown.

About the Author

Dr. Harold J. Sala is an internationally known radio personality, author, Bible teacher, lecturer, husband, and grandfather. His radio program, *Guidelines—A Five-Minute Commentary on Living*, is heard on more than 1000 stations in 17 languages and reaches into more than 100 countries; in the USA, it reaches 49 of the 50 states. It has been the recipient of the Catholic Mass Media Award for Moral Excellence in Broadcasting.

Dr. Sala holds a PhD in English Bible from Bob Jones University with proficiencies in Hebrew and Greek. His further graduate studies have been at the University of Southern California, California Baptist Seminary, Fuller Theological Seminary, and Denver Seminary.

More than 40 books and hundreds of publications have been authored by Dr. Sala, focusing on marriage, parenting, singles, counseling, and daily devotionals. His book *Heroes—People Who Have Changed the World* received the prestigious Angel Award for moral excellence in the media in the U.S. Dr. Sala has also been honored by CASA with the Heritage of Faithfulness Award. He serves on the boards of the Far East Broadcasting Company and the Friends of Donetsk Christian University, and he is chairman of the board of Joy Partners, a ministry to China.

His warm, personal style of sharing wisdom and insight from God's Word has brought hope to many. Dr. Sala is a frequent guest lecturer and teacher at many churches, schools, and international conferences, such as the Asian Theological Seminary in Manila and Donetsk Christian University in Ukraine, and the Ukrainian Institute for Artificial Intelligence.

His hobbies include golf, photography, and people—the driving focus of his life and ministry. Residing in California, Dr. Sala and his wife, Darlene, have three adult children and eight well-loved grandchildren.

Also by Harold J. Sala

WHEN YOUR HEART CRIES OUT TO GOD
Finding Comfort in Life's Trials

Wherever you are, whoever you are, God is there and He cares about you. In his straightforward, easy-to-understand way, author Harold Sala helps you see how this truth applies to a wide range of emotions and experiences. Concise selections include such topics as…

When You Want Peace
When You Suffer
When You Need Courage
When You Hope
When You Are Angry

When You Are Alone
When Your Broken Life Needs Healing
When You Are Frustrated
When You Need to Say, "I'm Sorry—
  Forgive Me"

---

*"Uplifting insights…Can be just the right message,
at just the right time."*

RICK WARREN
Author of *The Purpose-Driven Life*

WHY YOU CAN HAVE CONFIDENCE IN THE BIBLE
Bridging the Distance Between Your Heart and God's Word

Dr. Harold Sala presents fascinating evidence, personal stories, and illustrations that demonstrate why the Bible…

- is unique in what it says, who it speaks to, and how it's put together
- is interconnected with and supported by archaeology, astronomy, and other sciences
- shows you how to get across the chasms of meaning, relationships, ethics, or behavior in your life

Whether you're new to Scripture or experienced, here you'll find a bridge to exploring and applying the Bible in a way that will help you get to know its author better—which will change you for life. *Includes questions for thought and discussion.*

---

*"I commend Harold Sala's work to you
with much appreciation for his insight."*

RAVI ZACHARIAS
Author and Speaker

Other Books You'll Enjoy
from Harvest House

GOD'S BEST FOR MY LIFE
A Classic Daily Devotional

LLOYD JOHN OGILVIE

The bestselling daily guide to companionship with God.

As you meet with God day-by-day, His supernatural life will become real to you and in you. He will grant you His best for your life...

- friendship with Him that overcomes loneliness
- courage and endurance for life's challenges and adventures
- guidance when you're uncertain
- real love and affection for people—even those you have a tough time with
- inner peace that comes from the assurance He's always there

These 365 profoundly personal devotions invite you to discover, explore, and enjoy the incalculable blessing and love that wait for you when you spend time with the Father.

WALKIN' WITH GOD AIN'T FOR WIMPS
Spirit-Lifting Stories for the Young at Heart

KAREN O'CONNOR

Humorist Karen O'Connor reveals the joy, strength, and laughter that is ours when we walk with God...regardless of our circumstances. These short, real-life vignettes touch heart and soul, and they'll have you chuckling as you relate to the adventures and foibles of people just like you—or someone you know—and then share them with family and friends.

Each delightful tale concludes with an insightful Scripture and simple, life-affirming prayer that will remind you that God is with you in all ways—always!

GETTIN' OLD AIN'T FOR WIMPS

Inspirations and Stories to Warm Your Heart and Tickle Your Funny Bone

KAREN O'CONNOR

These lighthearted stories, inspiring Scriptures, and heartfelt prayers will make you grin and confess, "That sounds just like me!" Have you noticed that...

- when you can't find your glasses, they're usually on your head?
- the delightful honesty of youth sometimes bites?
- love still makes your heart skip a beat...or two...or three?

Gettin' Old Ain't for Wimps hilariously affirms that life will always be filled with wonder, promise, and adventure!

ANGELS IN THE ER

Inspiring True Stories from an Emergency Room Doctor

ROBERT LESSLIE, MD

If you don't believe in angels...you should spend some time in the ER. You'll learn that angels do exist. Some are nurses, a few are doctors, and many are everyday people.

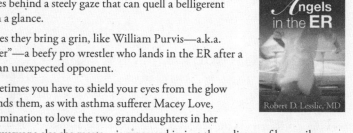

...Sometimes you have to look hard for their wings, as with well-starched head nurse Virginia Granger, whose heart of compassion hides behind a steely gaze that can quell a belligerent patient with a glance.

...Sometimes they bring a grin, like William Purvis—a.k.a. "Max Bruiser"—a beefy pro wrestler who lands in the ER after a tussle with an unexpected opponent.

...And sometimes you have to shield your eyes from the glow that surrounds them, as with asthma sufferer Macey Love, whose determination to love the two granddaughters in her care—and everyone else she meets—is expressed in just the radiance of her smile.

In these true stories—some thoughtful, some delightful, some heart-pumping—you'll see close-up the joys and struggles of people like you. Along with them, you can search your own heart for answers to finding grace and peace in the darkness, and living well in the light.

"A chronicle of mankind at its best."

RICHARD THOMAS

Film, TV, and stage actor; "John-Boy" on *The Waltons* and host of *It's a Miracle*

*To read a sample chapter of these or other Harvest House books,
go to www.harvesthousepublishers.com.*